"For many people, both inside and outside communities of faith, Christianity has become captive to blind allegiances that are driven more by fear than a concern for justice, more interested in building walls than expressing love and solidarity with neighbors who are different. If the church is going to break the stranglehold of these allegiances so that loyalty to Jesus and the kingdom he preached is placed back at the center of the life of faith, then the Pietist vision offered here will surely play an important role. Gehrz and Pattie offer a clear-eyed vision of faithful practice fired by the hope of the gospel that animated the original 'Pietist option,' and they do so without slavishly repeating seventeenth-century proposals. What is offered here is a compelling and practical vision that is geared toward our own contemporary challenges and context. This is a timely and much-needed work that should be warmly embraced by Christians from across the spectrum."

Christian T. Collins Winn, Bethel University, coauthor of *Reclaiming Pietism*

"Mark and Chris love God, the church, and the world. Here they ponder, *Does warmhearted Pietism have something to offer in a world of overheated debates?* This book offers no certain paths forward, but it does remind us that Pietism, with its emphases on a living personal faith, deep commitment to wanting to be guided by Scripture, engaging in mission to the world, and generous fellowship, just might have something to offer."

Gary Walter, president of the Evangelical Covenant Church

"This is a timely book. The issues that led to the Pietist movement are present in different forms in the church today. Church attendance and participation are declining. A growing portion of the emerging generation finds little value in what the church seems to offer. For many, the evangelical expression of the church has become a political movement more than a source of life-giving hope. This book offers an alternative with roots in an earlier movement where faith is a relationship, not merely a philosophy of life. The following quote from the book captures the essence: 'That's primarily how Pietists know God: not through propositions (what we believe about the idea of God), but prepositions (how we relate to the person of God), as we experience a living faith *through* Jesus Christ, who is Emmanuel, God *with* us.'"

Glenn R. Palmberg, president emeritus, Evangelical Covenant Church

"*The Pietist Option* is historically faithful, biblically rooted, and encouraging. Christopher Gehrz and Mark Pattie III help us see how Christ-followers in past centuries faced challenging issues in ways that are relevant to current events. Gehrz has meaningfully elevated Bethel University's Pietist roots to current day relevance as we commit to engage the world's most challenging problems, to God's glory and for our neighbors' good. *The Pietist Option* has wisdom for the church, the academy, and the neighborhood. I'm thankful for this resource."

Jay Barnes, president, Bethel University

THE PIETIST OPTION

Hope for the Renewal
of Christianity

Christopher Gehrz and Mark Pattie III

IVP Academic

An imprint of InterVarsity Press
Downers Grove, Illinois

InterVarsity Press
P.O. Box 1400, Downers Grove, IL 60515-1426
ivpress.com
email@ivpress.com

*InterVarsity Press® is the book-publishing division of InterVarsity Christian Fellowship/USA®, a movement of
students and faculty active on campus at hundreds of universities, colleges, and schools of nursing in the United States
of America, and a member movement of the International Fellowship of Evangelical Students. For information about
local and regional activities, visit intervarsity.org.*

Cover design: Faceout Studio, Derek Thornton
Interior design: Daniel van Loon

ISBN 978-0-8308-5194-2 (print)
ISBN 978-0-8308-8911-2 (digital)

Printed in the United States of America ♾

*InterVarsity Press is committed to ecological stewardship and to the conservation of natural resources in all our
operations. This book was printed using sustainably sourced paper.*

Library of Congress Cataloging-in-Publication Data
A catalog record for this book is available from the Library of Congress.

P	21	20	19	18	17	16	15	14	13	12	11	10	9	8	7	6	5	4	3	2	1
Y	34	33	32	31	30	29	28	27	26	25	24	23	22	21	20	19	18	17

Dedicated to the memory of
James R. Hawkinson and Glen V. Wiberg,
who lived the Pietist option and so taught it to others.

"Think of us in this way,
as servants of Christ and
stewards of God's mysteries."
1 CORINTHIANS 4:1

Contents

Introduction

"Come Back to Jesus"

After a long day attending a Christian conference full of lively worship, big-name speakers, and a multitude of workshops, I (Mark) was exhausted. I'd been taking notes all day long. Five steps to this, ten to that. How to pastor, lead, worship, teach, strategize, evangelize—whatever it is you want to do, with these few steps you can do it better. And Lord knows, there are plenty of things I'd like to improve on. I took copious notes.

Late that night, after I'd been asleep for several hours, I had a dream in which I looked up and heard God speaking to me. "Mark!" God called.

"Yes, Lord," I answered.

"Do you want to know the steps to a vital life and a vital church?"

"Yes, Lord! Yes!" I exclaimed. And in my dream I grabbed the notebook I'd been carrying around all day, took out a pencil, and wrote "Steps to a Vital Life and a Vital Church" at the top of a blank page and then a number one just under the heading. I looked up with anticipation.

"Come back to Jesus," God said.

"Come back to Jesus," I wrote. Then, penciling in a number two on the line below, I looked up again to hear the next step.

And I woke up.

"No!" I exclaimed to myself and to God. "Please, Lord! What is number two, and three, and four? What are the rest of the steps?"

But there was no answer, no way to get back into the dream, no way to go back to sleep for quite a while. "Come back to Jesus" was all I heard.

After getting up, I spent the day at the conference attending yet more seminars, but my head and heart were elsewhere, thinking, praying, and wondering about the dream.

It wasn't until later, as I listened to the evening concert, that it struck me: there is no step number two, or three, or four. Just this one. Always this one. "Come back to Jesus."

Movements of the Holy Spirit

Again and again through the centuries there have been fresh movements of the Holy Spirit to bring new life to the church and new hope to the world. For all their complexities, at the heart of every one of these movements has been this simple call to come back to Jesus: to center our lives, relationships, ministries, and mission clearly and consistently on him who alone is the way, the truth, and the life (Jn 14:6).

Five centuries ago one such movement took shape in central Europe: the Reformation. Martin Luther and other Protestant Reformers preached salvation by grace alone, translated the Bible into the languages of everyday life, and encouraged all believers to see themselves as part of a common priesthood. At the same time, their Catholic brethren experienced their own reformation thanks to innovative leaders such as Ignatius Loyola, whose Jesuits founded schools and universities in Europe and brought the gospel to Asia and the Americas.

By the late seventeenth century, such reforming energy had been spent. Instead Christians fought each other in a series of wars that left behind competing churches more concerned with maintaining doctrinal boundaries than encouraging evangelism, spiritual growth, or social reform. But once again a new movement emerged to turn Christians back to Christ. It was called Pietism.

Historians credit the Pietists' warm-hearted devotion to Jesus with reviving the cold, harsh, bickering Christianity of the time. While it started in what's now Germany, Pietism's influence could be felt around the world, from India to Greenland, England to the Caribbean. Some scholars even suggest connections with African American Christianity and the global movement of Pentecostalism. Now, over three hundred years later, we believe that the spirit of Pietism can again help Christians come back to Jesus, as God once more renews his church and revitalizes its witness to the world.

Pietism as Movement and Ethos

A couple summers ago I (Chris) took a trip to Iowa's Rathbun Lake for a reunion of my wife's family. It's a part of the state whose chief claim to fame in American religious history is that Mormon pioneers passed through in 1846 en route to the Great Salt Lake. But that landscape is also dotted with artifacts of Pietism, what theologian Roger Olson says was once "*the* main form of Protestantism" on this continent.

Even if you lived there, you might not think of Appanoose County as a historic center of Pietism. How many people in the town of Moravia (population 665) know that its founders were part of a movement that had been reenergized in the eighteenth century by a Pietist aristocrat named Nikolaus von Zinzendorf, the godson of Philipp Jakob Spener, the founder of German Pietism? Or that a Methodist church stands at the corner of North and William Streets because one day in 1738 an Anglican priest named John Wesley felt his heart "strangely warmed" while attending a Moravian meeting in London? How many of the Brethren who gather at a white-washed church nestled in the cornfields south of Unionville, or their Grace Brethren cousins who used to meet in nearby Udell, can tell the story of their founder, Alexander Mack, who fused Pietism and Anabaptism thirty years before Wesley's conversion?

For some, this is Pietism: a chapter in church history that has closed, leaving behind aging artifacts and obscure answers to trivia questions. Pietism, according to its Wikipedia entry, "had almost vanished in America by the end of the 20th century."

We're convinced there's a bright future in all that hidden history, but this summary does point out how, as a *movement*, Pietism flared brightly in late seventeenth- and early eighteenth-century Germany, then faded away. Suspicious of faith becoming too institutional or too intellectual,

> Pietism has disappeared not because it failed, but because it *succeeded*.

Pietists did not generate the denominational structures or doctrinal documents that would have set up their movement for long-term survival.

But here's the crucial point: Pietism has disappeared not because it failed, but because it *succeeded*. Mennonite historian Steve Nolt describes Pietism as "leavening" later religious movements such as the Grace Brethren. It's an insightful, Jesus-style, kingdom of God–revealing metaphor (see Mt 13:33). In bread making yeast does its magic subtly, bringing out the potential of the other ingredients while leaving little of its own presence behind. Likewise, Pietism can work its way into a Christian movement, enhancing what's already there while leaving few traces of itself.

This moves us away from thinking of Pietism as a particular historical *movement* that came with Spener and Mack and went with Zinzendorf and Wesley. Instead, it points to Pietism as a timeless *spirit*, or *ethos*. "This ethos," write Roger Olson and Christian Collins Winn, "transcends denominations and even traditions: it 'pops up' in all kinds of Christian movements, organizations, and individuals." What they say of Zinzendorf's intention for his movement we would claim for Pietism in our time: "Moravianism existed to renew the whole church, and should it succeed, it would pass away, having fulfilled its calling."

As an ethos that leavens different flavors of Christianity, Pietism has proven to be remarkably adaptable. Baptist historian Virgil Olson doubted that Pietism could be "perpetuated" for very long. But he trusted that the spirit of Pietism would regain its strength whenever people grew dissatisfied with "superficial Christianity whether it be found in rotting formalism, a thinned-out evangelism or a misfired scholasticism, or anything else that has the form of piety and lacks the power thereof [2 Tim 3:5]." In other words, Pietism calls people back to Jesus when and where it's most needed—whether seventeenth-century Germany or twenty-first-century America.

We know this firsthand because we participate in religious movements that have not only been leavened by the Pietist ethos in the past but are returning to it in the present. First, Mark and I are members of the Evangelical Covenant Church (ECC or Covenant), founded in 1885 by Swedish immigrants who had been part of a pietistic revival in the Lutheran state church back home. (And yes, I found a Covenant church on my tour of Pietist Iowa, a stately old building in Centerville.) While the ECC of the twenty-first century is a multiethnic denomination, its current president rarely misses a chance to remind Covenanters of all backgrounds that we are "missional Pietists."

> Pietism calls people back to Jesus when and where it's most needed—whether seventeenth-century Germany or twenty-first-century America.

In addition, I work at Bethel University, founded in 1871 by Swedish Baptists who emerged from the same revival as did the Covenant Church. In the past decade that university has been recovering its Pietist heritage. In 2015, for example, I brought together current and former Bethel colleagues to write *The Pietist Vision of Christian Higher Education: Forming Whole and Holy Persons*.

So what is it that makes these more recent movements "Pietist"? If it's an adaptable ethos that changes with its conditions, how do we know what Pietism is and what it isn't?

Pietism as Instincts

Some identify Pietism with shared practices (personal devotions, small group meetings, evangelism, charitable work) or shared emphases (conversion, right feeling and action prioritized over right belief, ecumenism, a greater role for the laity). There's something to both approaches, but we want to propose something a bit different: *Pietists share certain instincts.*

These instincts aren't even settled beliefs, just impulses or inclinations. They start in the heart before they reach the head. They're not always right, and they don't always fit well together. But when presented with a new situation, Pietists would most likely respond in one or more of the following ways.

We know God more through prepositions than propositions. Biblical faith has always been about relationships, beginning with the most central one of all, our relationship with God. "Where are you?" God called out in the garden (Gen 3:9), and ever since, the question of where we are in relationship to God has been the essential one for each person and generation. If we come back to Jesus, the Son of God, we come back to a relationship.

The late, great British evangelical John Stott structured one of his books, *Life in Christ*, around aspects of this relationship. With each chapter focused on a certain aspect of Jesus Christ and how we relate to him, Stott fleshed out what it means to live *under* Christ our Lord, *like* Christ our model, *on* Christ our foundation, and so on.

That's primarily how Pietists know God: not through propositions (what we believe about the idea of God) but through prepositions (how we relate to the person of God). We experience a living faith *through* Jesus Christ, who is Emmanuel, God *with* us. Pietism, says historian Alec Ryrie, "was a rekindling of the love affair with God that had been Protestantism's beating heart since Luther."

Of course, what we believe about God matters. Christians don't strive to become more like just any model, but an incarnate one; build their church on just any foundation, but a resurrected one; or live under just any Lord, but an ascended one who will return again as Judge. Intellectual propositions are needed.

But they're not enough. Before we attempt to make theological sense of God and after intellectual certainty gives way to mystery and paradox, we experience life in, with, through, under, and for God. Christians who lose sight of this, who crave the certainty of fixed propositions, risk sliding into what Pietists call "dead orthodoxy."

We're better together than apart. You can tell a lot about a Christian by looking at her Bible: some passages have been read so often that the Good Book falls open to them. For many Mennonites, it's the Sermon on the Mount; for many Calvinists, a favorite chapter in Romans. Pietists come time and again to John 17, meditating on how Jesus prays to his Father:

I ask not only on behalf of these, but also on behalf of those who will believe in me through their word, that they may all be one. As you, Father, are in me and I am in you, may they also be in us, so that the world may believe that you have sent me. The glory that you have given me I have given them, so that they may be one, as we are one, I in them and you in me, that they may become completely one, so that the world may know that you have sent me and have loved them even as you have loved me. (Jn 17:20-23)

Again, relationships matter! As much as Pietists yearn for loving intimacy with God (one more preposition: "As you . . . are *in* me and I am *in* you, may they also be *in* us"), they desire close relationships with those made in God's image. But to Pietists' dismay, Jesus' call to unity ("that they may be one, as we are one") has often gone unheeded by Christians who can't agree with each other about propositions. As we'll argue in chapter six, that failure has dire implications for Christian witness and mission ("so that the world may believe . . . so that the world may know").

Christianity is both less and more than we think. This is a play on the first instinct: Pietists who live in, with, and for the person of Jesus probably *feel* his presence more than they *think* about the idea of Christ. But they also tend to suspect that if we answer the call to "Come back to Jesus," we'll soon find that being a Christ-follower is both less and more than what we've assumed.

Less because if those four words are the call, then there's a good chance that we've made Christianity too complicated. So Pietists simplify. For example, their lists of essential doctrines tend to be short. Our denomination has just six affirmations, the last of which is that we're free to disagree on other matters that are not essential to salvation. *Less* also in that Pietists do not place their faith in the same scales the never-satisfied world uses to measure success. They know that authentic Christianity cannot be coerced through political power or social pressure, or enticed through cultural relevance or economic incentives. It requires a free response to that fundamental call: "Come back to Jesus."

More in that answering that call leads to growth, to change so radical that we can only start to describe it with two of the New Testament's most audacious metaphors: new birth (Jn 3:7) and new life (e.g., Rom 6:4). Pietists fully expect the encounter with Jesus to be transformative. (Not that such change happens all at once for every person! Unlike his successor, August Hermann Francke, Spener never described, let alone dated, the kind of Damascus Road conversion experience that became a model for so many evangelicals.) While Luther was right to expect that saints will always remain, to some degree, sinners, his Pietist heirs know that the Protestant Reformer was on to something when he gushed, "O it is a living, busy, active, mighty thing, this faith. It is impossible for it not to be doing good works incessantly."

We always have hope for better times. If God can transform the life of an individual, Pietists trust that he can do the same for the larger church and the world beyond it. Even when the recent and distant past make it seem likely that dismal patterns will continue, Pietists understand that the central event in human history is not the fall of Adam but the resurrection of Jesus. God disrupts all patterns, makes all things new (Rev 21:5). As a resurrection people, Pietists actively expect that God will continue to break into the world in unexpected ways, bringing new life where otherwise there is death.

A God known more through prepositions than propositions, a commitment to stay together, a Christianity that is less and more than we think, and an enduring hope for better times. Like any instincts, these four are fallible. We must always test such impulsive responses against Scripture and subject them to careful thought, or else twenty-first-century Pietists may go as far astray as some of their predecessors. It's not entirely unfair that in some Christian circles Pietism is synonymous with legalism, Pharisaism, sentimentalism, anti-intellectualism, or "being too heavenly minded to do earthly good." But if you've felt our four instincts flicker in

> If God can transform the life of an individual, Pietists trust that he can do the same for the larger church and the world beyond it.

your own heart, you should consider what we might call the Pietist option for the renewal of Christianity.

The Pietist Option

Why "option"? As I've written elsewhere, we're talking about a kind of Christianity that is "not inherited or assumed, coerced or affected." Pietism doesn't happen accidentally; it requires a conscious choice to respond to God's grace. The Pietist option is to *opt in* to a distinctively hopeful way of coming back to Jesus: growing to be more and more like him, living at peace as part of his body, and fulfilling his mission in service to others.

Just know that the aim of this book is not to produce Pietists! We're convinced that there are tremendous resources available in the rich history of the Pietist movement and ethos that will leaven your faith, which has no doubt been shaped and sustained by other experiences and traditions. Like its alternatives, the Pietist option has its own strengths and weaknesses. And like other such options, it's a means to a much greater end.

When God calls each of us back to Jesus, he also calls us back to our roles as members of the body of Christ. So our hope is that people who share some or all of our four Pietist instincts will come away from this book better equipped to fulfill what we Covenanters call the *whole mission of the church*: making disciples of all nations, followers of Jesus Christ who make their faith active in love through ministries of compassion and justice. In fact, we're at our most missional when, in words our denomination explicitly attributes to our Pietist roots, we "hold together proclamation and compassion, personal witness and social justice, service and stewardship in all areas of life."

Why Christianity could use some new resources and new energy in fulfilling this mission will be the focus of chapter one, while chapter two will explain why Pietists approach their work with such deep-seated hope. Then the remaining chapters will offer six practical proposals for the renewal of individuals and—through them—the church and the world.

Readers already familiar with Pietist history will recognize this structure. It mirrors the organization of Philipp Spener's *Pia Desideria*, the short book that launched the German Pietist movement in 1675. Indeed, several of Spener's "pious wishes" remain timely today. For us as for Spener, Christianity is more about life than mere belief (chapter five). Like him, we believe that no revival is likely to go anywhere if it doesn't start with ordinary Christians listening to the transformative Word of God in the written word of Scripture (chapter three), and that we ought to avoid needless controversies and focus on what unites Christians (chapter six).

But we're not simply rehashing seventeenth-century advice; *Pia Desideria* is a starting point, not a destination. Even when we address the same themes as Spener (also including the role of laypeople in chapter four, education in chapter seven, and preaching in chapter eight), we don't expect the problems or the solutions in 2017 to be precisely what they were in 1675. At least in part that difference is because the option introduced by Spener has now been around for more than three hundred years. It has inspired a great deal of wise reflection and application, supplying more resources from the past that we can retrieve for the future.

In particular, we want to share the stories of the Evangelical Covenant Church and Bethel University, which both began two centuries after Spener and remain little known in the larger church. We'll mention other examples of Pietist leavening, but if you were to show people what it looks like to choose the Pietist option in contemporary America—for better and for worse—you couldn't do much better than to show them Bethel and the Covenant.

At its core, however, the nature of the Pietist option has not changed drastically since Spener addressed *Pia Desideria* to his readers:

> With sincere devotion let us therefore help one another to wrestle with prayer and supplication, that here and there God may open up one door after another to his Word, that we may proclaim the mystery of Christ fruitfully, that we may do so cheerfully and speak in a befitting manner, and that we may glorify his name with our teaching, our life, and our suffering.

Like him and all Pietists since, we write in the midst of adversity as people of the resurrection, calling people to come back to the One who overcame sin, death, and evil. May you finish this book enlivened and empowered by the Spirit of our risen Lord, Jesus Christ, confident that we can hope for better times.

A brief word about how this book is written and with whose help. First, as with one of Chris's earlier works, we wanted *The Pietist Option* to be "Pietist not just in content but tone." No matter the topic, for example, we hope that you sense the "irenic spirit" that Chris discusses in chapter six. Further, our background in the Covenant means that we always write with two questions in the back of our minds. One, "Where is it written?" leads us to turn again and again to Scripture, which is not only our "only perfect rule for faith, doctrine, and conduct" but an "altar where we meet the living God" (as Mark will explain in chapter three). The other, "How goes your walk with Christ?" prompts us to tell stories arising from this journey, at least as often as we make arguments. After all, Pietists have been sharing personal testimonies since Johanna Eleonora Petersen wrote her spiritual memoir in the late seventeenth century.

Second, you'll note two rather distinctive voices taking turns: Chris primarily wrote chapters one, four, six, and seven, plus most of this introduction; Mark took chapters two, three, five, and eight, plus the book's benediction. One voice will sound more like that of a pastor; the other, a college professor. And we don't necessarily agree on every point. But every chapter reflects months and years of conversations between us, and hopefully you'll hear us continuing to speak with each other across these pages.

To us, this approach seems appropriate to a religious ethos that cherishes conversation and insists that not even the preacher's voice ought to predominate in the life of a congregation. As we'll mention at several points in the following pages, German Pietism helped to popularize the small groups that now appear in most all Christian churches.

Indeed, the content of this book has already been shaped by a kind of digital-age conventicle. Over the course of twelve podcast episodes in early 2016, we thought aloud through each chapter; on air we bounced ideas off each other and our friend Sam Mulberry, then so-licited feedback from listeners via social media. Later Chris shared rough drafts of selected chapters on his blog to get some last-minute comments from potential readers before the manuscript shipped off to the publisher. Among our other acknowledgments, we're grateful to Sam and all the other listeners and readers whose voices echoed in our ears while we were writing.

We were also in literal or figurative conversation with many other students of Pietism, some of whose words you'll see quoted in the pages to come. Our errors in this work are our own, but our ideas have been shaped by scholars and pastors living and dead, including Phil Anderson, Jason Barnhart, Dale Brown, G. W. Carlson, Michelle Clifton-Soderstrom, Christian Collins Winn, Don Frisk, Jim Hawkinson, Carl Lundquist, Roger Olson, Karl Olsson, Steve Pitts, John Weborg, and Glen Wiberg. In addition, Susan Pattie helped her brother tell the story of the Armenian genocide in chapters two and five.

Both of us are deeply indebted to the congregation, leadership team, and staff of Salem Covenant Church for their encouragement and support throughout this project. And of course we are so very grateful for the efforts of two editors: David Congdon, who helped us get this project off the ground, and Jon Boyd, who saw it through to completion.

Finally, we can but begin to thank Donna, Lauren, Mark, Jonathan, Katie, Lena, Isaiah, and the rest of our families, who remind us daily that "the only thing that counts is faith working through love" (Gal 5:6).

PART ONE

Christianity in the Early Twenty-First Century

CHAPTER 1

What's Wrong?

Mark and I will have a lot to say about hope for better times in this book, just as Pietist pioneer Philipp Spener did in his *Pia Desideria*. But the book that helped launch the German Pietist movement in 1675 begins on a darker note, with a prophet's grief:

O that my head were a spring of water,
    and my eyes a fountain of tears,
so that I might weep day and night
    for the slain of my poor people! (quoting Jer 9:1)

Hopeful as he was, Spener even borrowed words from the second-century martyr Polycarp ("Good God, for what times hast thou preserved me!") to underscore the seriousness of seventeenth-century problems: "In our day we have much more reason to repeat such words, or rather to sigh them, for the greater the distress the more one is at a loss for words."

Some of the "corrupt conditions" that Spener decried in *Pia Desideria* would be familiar to Christians now; some would not. Writing in the aftermath of a particularly ugly presidential election, I want to nod along with his dismal description of political leaders: "few of them know what Christianity is, to say nothing of their being Christians and practicing the Christian life." But we need to recognize that he had in mind a vastly different kind of political system. Some of Spener's opening complaints we would rather not mention at all, such as the anti-Catholic vitriol that was typical of Lutherans who still saw the papacy as "the anti-Christian Babel."

Whether or not we echo his specific concerns, Mark and I wouldn't be writing this book if we didn't think that there's still need for reform and revival. So we'll join Spener in starting with a sampling of what's wrong, in the hope that "the complaints of godly people . . . should encourage one another and promote the work of the Lord ever more earnestly than before."

But First . . .

I wish I didn't have to write this chapter! In my experience, the worst part of any Christian book is the one that explains what's wrong with the church. First, even ten chapters like this couldn't cover every problem that deserves attention. Second, by the time this book is published, any take on current events will be stale. Third, and most troubling to me, it seems that the only thing easier than criticizing Christianity is promoting your own book as offering all the solutions to the religion's problems. (That, or dismissing religion altogether and claiming that Jesus is best followed apart from anything like an institutional church or a historical tradition.)

We do believe that the Pietist option holds out great promise for renewal. But in this chapter I don't want to make it sound like the only really important issues are those that Pietism happens to address most clearly. Sometimes those dots will connect, but we also want to be honest about the pitfalls of Pietism—and to acknowledge when its history has little to offer us today but awkward silence. And if we do need to stand in judgment on Christianity today, we still want to evoke the irenic spirit and humble posture of the Pietists who have inspired us, not the self-righteousness that is also part of that tradition.

So I've tried to take to heart some advice that Mark shared early on in our process. He told me that he prepares to write his sermons by first asking God, "What's your word *for me*? And then what's your word *through me*? What can I share with others that may be helpful, by the grace of your Spirit?" So before I made bold to write about what ails the church and the world, I asked God to help me understand better what ails me.

Such prayerful self-examination is deeply embedded in the Pietist tradition. Spener's most famous follower, August Hermann Francke, believed that new birth first required an intense struggle with sin (in German, *Busskampf*) that led to repentance:

Just as the seed strewn upon the naked surface of the earth can bring no fruit unless the field is first well plowed and fertilized . . . so must the human, evil heart be well plowed by the plow of the Law, that man may learn to know the old sins, evil habits, and preconceived notions in which he stands, take fright at it, be broken and crushed in his heart over it, and bring before God the Lord true remorse and suffering for it.

> If we're seeking after renewal, it's got to start with you and me confessing how we've failed to love God and to love our neighbors.

I didn't experience the depths of Francke's sorrow ("This misery brought many tears from my eyes") or the ecstasy of his conversion ("I was suddenly so overwhelmed as with a stream of joy"), but I think his advice is still sound: "Chastise yourself first before you chastise others, so that your chastisement proceeds from compassion."

Not surprisingly, God had many words of chastisement for me, only some of which might flow through me in the pages I have left in this chapter. But in the end, all those words call us back to the Word, Jesus Christ, whose greatest commandment is the standard for all that we do as his followers: "You shall love the Lord your God with all your heart, and with all your soul, and with all your mind, and with all your strength. . . . You shall love your neighbor as yourself" (Mk 12:30-31). If we're seeking after renewal, it's got to start with you and me confessing how we've failed to love God and to love our neighbors.

Functional Atheism

Oppression upon oppression, deceit upon deceit! They refuse to know me, says the LORD.

JEREMIAH 9:6

Pietists like to contrast "living faith" with "dead orthodoxy." And what orthodoxy could be deader than to *know* that God exists yet too often *act* as if he were absent? If "fools say in their hearts, 'There is no God'" (Ps 14:1), I'd hate to hear what the psalmist would say of me, who readily proclaims his belief in God but too rarely pauses to read God's Word, pray to him, or simply adore him in silent contemplation. Rather than coming back to a life-giving relationship with God, I act like Adam and Eve, who "hid themselves from the presence of the LORD" (Gen 3:8).

I can't count all the times I've pledged to break this pattern and re-commit to the kinds of devotional habits that have been so important to so many Pietists. Yet again and again I stop and realize that I've been spending my time frenetically, trying to cram as much work as possible into my waking hours. That I even use the phrase "*spending* my time" suggests how completely I've accommodated to the priorities and rhythms of a human economy, rather than participating in a divine one. Too often I act as if *efficiency* and *productivity*, not *fruitfulness* and *rest*, were biblical values and not corporate buzzwords.

The centerpiece of God's economy is sabbath. However we choose to keep holy some part of our week, Lauren Winner wants us to remember that authentic sabbath keeping is not motivated by "what we might call capitalism's justification. . . . Rest for the sake of future productivity is at odds with the spirit of Shabbat." Instead, this holy rest honors God and strengthens our relationship with him. Think prepositions again: in sabbath, Winner writes, we give our life *to* God and seek to become more *like* him.

Winner repeats advice from an eighteenth-century Pietist, Johann Friedrich Stark, that the Christian should pray and rest on Saturday night in order to "disentangle his mind from worldly cares and troubles" and prepare for Sunday. It's counsel I need to heed, and probably more than one evening a week. (Stark advises a "daily or spiritual sabbath . . . a daily laying aside of our sins" in preparation for our "eternal Sabbath in the life to come.") If I don't spend time—unproductive, restful, in-efficient, fruitful time—with God, I not only act as if he didn't exist, but I continue to "conform to the pattern of this world" (Rom 12:2 NIV) rather than striving first for God's kingdom.

Why do I find it so hard to break this pattern? Perhaps because working as hard as I can (and praying as little as I do) leaves me feeling like I'm in control—not a subject of God's kingdom but a ruler of my own. And that points to another kind of lifeless belief, what the Quaker educator Parker Palmer calls "functional atheism": "the belief that ultimate responsibility for everything rests with us. . . . The unconscious, unexamined conviction that if anything decent is going to happen here, we are the ones who must make it happen—a conviction held even by people who talk a good game about God." For all that I want to say in this book about the virtue of hope, it's shocking to realize how often I act as though the only future open is the one that I can bring about by my efforts in accordance with my vision. And how easily I fall into sleepless fretting when that future doesn't materialize quickly enough.

Let's go back once more to sabbath. Winner (a convert from Orthodox Judaism) notes that as Christians keep it—on the Easter of each week—sabbath "commemorates not only God's resting from Creation, but also God's Resurrection." But does our belief in this miracle make any difference in how we live? Are we the faithful followers of a risen Christ who said, "Peace be with you" (Jn 20:19), or more like the disbelieving disciples who responded to an unsealed tomb by locking their doors?

Consider a June 2016 survey. The Pew Research Center asked over 2,200 Americans which issues were "very important" as they looked ahead to the presidential election. What mattered most to the Christians most like me? Not education, the environment, or the economy; not even abortion or the Supreme Court. No, 89 percent of white evangelicals said that terrorism was "very important." No other religious group was so likely to emphasize that issue, and religious "nones" were much less concerned about terrorist attack. I don't mean to suggest that our country shouldn't protect itself. But according to an analysis by a conservative think tank, the chances of an American being killed by a foreign terrorist are over three million to one!

"Be strong and courageous," Joshua told the Israelites; "do not be frightened or dismayed, for the LORD your God is with you wherever you go" (Josh 1:9). Yet how many times have Christians like me quoted that verse and still lived in fear, as if Pentecost brought the church "a spirit of cowardice" rather than "a spirit of power and of love and of self-discipline" (2 Tim 1:7)? There's a difference between prudence and fearfulness. Yet the people who bear the name of the evangel, the good news, can seem the most fearful. The same people who argue most strenuously for the historicity of the resurrection can seem the least likely to live as if Jesus Christ has actually conquered the grave.

> The same people who argue most strenuously for the historicity of the resurrection can seem the least likely to live as if Jesus Christ has actually conquered the grave.

Scripture attests to a faithful, powerful God who is "making all things new" (Rev 21:5), but fear of what's to come tempts us to make God in our own image: beset by our anxieties, vexed by our worries, frustrated by our grievances, and confined by our limitations. And if that's the God we worship, then we're not just engaging in the dead orthodoxy of functional atheism, we're practicing the most selfish, destructive kind of idolatry: exalting the fears of our mortal selves instead of believing in the resurrected Son of God and thereby having "life in his name" (Jn 20:31).

Love Without Justice, Justice Without Grace

The commandments, "You shall not commit adultery; You shall not murder; You shall not steal; You shall not covet"; and any other commandment, are summed up in this word, "Love your neighbor as yourself."

ROMANS 13:9

Some Pietists have been so committed to cultivating their personal, private relationship with God that they have been "too heavenly minded to be earthly good." But in my study of Pietist movements and my experience of the ethos, such otherworldliness is fairly uncommon.

Most Pietists have understood that faith comes most alive in love of neighbor. "If we can . . . awaken a fervent love among our Christians," wrote Spener in *Pia Desideria*, "first toward one another and then toward all men . . . and put this love into practice, practically all that we desire will be accomplished." In this respect, as in so many others, Spener simply thought that Pietism was reviving the principles of Martin Luther, who wrote, "Faith brings you to Christ and makes Him your own with all that He has; Love gives you to your neighbor with all that you have." According to Francke, some Lutherans let their aversion to "works-righteousness" lead them to "think it is not even their duty to do good," to the point that he threatened, "if the Lutheran doctrine brought this . . . may we renounce it forever." Not just "God's glory" but "neighbor's good" was the purpose of the new life for Francke.

But too many of us tend to substitute another word for love—like the translators who rendered Paul's most famous statement of Christian virtue this way: "And now abideth faith, hope, charity, these three; but the greatest of these is charity" (1 Cor 13:13 KJV). There is nothing wrong with charity, but love for neighbor demands that we seek justice for our neighbor. I might summon the empathy required to feed the hungry and welcome the stranger (Mt 25:35), but God also requires that I ask where that deprivation and alienation came from—and what I can do to stop them from happening again.

And those aren't always comfortable questions for a Christian like me. White, male, upper middle class, PhD holding, and American, I reap enormous advantages from the same racial, gender, economic, educational, and global inequalities that disadvantage most of humanity. All that privilege can distract me from what N. T. Wright calls "the echo of a voice: a voice speaking with calm, healing authority, speaking about justice, about things being put to rights, about peace and hope and prosperity for all."

In part, that's why so many Christians like me like to recall a supposed golden age of our nation's history, when churches seemed fuller, the economy seemed stronger, and our politics seemed less divisive. In its 2015 American Values Survey, the Public Religion Research Institute found that 60 percent of white evangelicals and 56 percent of white mainline Protestants believed that America's best days were behind it. While majorities of all other religious groups looked forward expectantly to America's future, white Protestants looked back wistfully at a nostalgic past, prompting Southern Baptist leader Russell Moore to chastise them for "blinding themselves to the injustices faced by their black and brown brothers and sisters in the supposedly idyllic Mayberry of white Christian America."

We're still blinding ourselves to such injustices. All lives do matter, but white Christians find it far too easy to ignore the many ways in which our racialized society continues to diminish black lives. Consider the rash of officer-involved shootings that have left African American men dead. "Many white evangelicals," observed Moore, "will . . . argue that the particulars are more complex in those situations than initial news reports might show. But how can anyone deny, after seeing the sheer number of cases and after seeing those in which the situation is all too clear, that there is a problem in terms of the safety of African-Americans before the law." He was responding to a July 2016 case when a Minnesota policeman shot and killed Philando Castile during a traffic stop. That incident took place only a mile from my house—but a world away from my own experience. As Moore concluded, "Such injustices are so longstanding and are often hidden from majority populations, who don't pay attention to such questions because they rarely have to think about them."

At the same time, when my eyes do open, when my ears do somehow perk up at Wright's "echo of a voice," I tend to answer with angry self-righteousness. I forget that the Lord demands not only that I "do justice" but that I "love kindness" and "walk humbly with [my] God" (Mic 6:8). Most importantly, I neglect grace, what Philip Yancey calls "Christianity's best gift to the world, a spiritual nova in our midst exerting a force stronger than vengeance, stronger than racism, stronger than hate." But grace, he admits, is also a "scandal," starting with the "unnatural act of forgiveness." Practicing grace comes even less easily than doing justice; indeed, it often runs counter to what we think and feel to be just. Yet I can hardly love my neighbor as myself if I'm unwilling to forgive either my neighbor or myself when we act unjustly, cruelly, or arrogantly.

So while it can be helpful to engage in something like Francke's *Busskampf* and contemplate both personal and social sin, Pietists' emphasis on repentance has sometimes misled them into austere legalism. For example, Yancey interprets the Isak Dinesen story "Babette's Feast" as a parable of grace revitalizing a pietistic Scandinavian sect that had joylessly "tried to earn God's favor with their pieties and renunciations."

But at its best, the Pietist option starts with the decision to be honest about our failures to love God and neighbor (again, "as yourself"), in the hope that we will grow in God's grace. In her book on Pietist ethics, Michelle Clifton-Soderstrom illustrates the virtue of love by telling of the remarkable Johanna Eleonora Petersen, who not only led a Pietist community in the late seventeenth century but taught and even preached. Petersen went through her own *Busskampf,* but she addressed "sin within the narrative of the gospel—a gospel that both confronts and forgives." Clifton-Soderstrom concludes by passing along wisdom from one of her mentors, Covenant theologian John Weborg: "Fear, for [Pietists], was never about terror of God's wrath or punishment; rather, it was the fear of *not* grasping the gift of God's free grace as a precious gift."

> The Pietist option starts with the decision to be honest about our failures to love God and neighbor, in the hope that we will grow in God's grace.

And Who Is My Neighbor?

"One of Jesus' clearest teachings," writes Clifton-Soderstrom, the commandment to love God and neighbor, "gives life and breath to our faith." Like many Christians, I know it by heart. But the verse that I'm actually best at living out is the question that follows in Luke's account: "And who is my neighbor?" (Lk 10:29).

Like the lawyer who first tested Jesus and then to tried to justify himself, I'd rather redirect God's attention away from my failure to love others by quibbling about the very term *neighbor*. I make little effort to know the people living next door and across the street. Surely, I tell myself, following Jesus can't realistically compel me to love neighbors separated from me not just by a fence or street but by class, education, race, language, sexuality, or political ideology.

Like a growing number of Americans, I've redefined *neighbor* in a most unbiblical way. Consider this dismal summary from Paul Taylor of the Pew Research Center: "In an era of head-snapping racial, social, cultural, economic, religious, gender, generational and technological change, Americans are increasingly sorted into think-alike communities that reflect not only their politics but their demographics. . . . It's as if they belong not to rival parties but alien tribes." Increasingly, we have different values based on different sources of information and lived out in relationship with different groups of people. On social media we block, mute, and unfollow those who irritate or criticize us, even as sophisticated algorithms sift the news we read and the arguments we consider. But it's not just a virtual problem. Taylor noted that we're even living in different places, with liberals favoring cities and conservatives preferring small towns and rural areas.

If it wasn't clear before, this sorting into "alien tribes" became obvious in the 2016 presidential election, when over 60 percent of voters lived in a county where a single candidate—either Donald Trump or Hillary Clinton—won over 60 percent of the vote. "That's up from 50 percent of voters who lived in such counties in 2012 and 39 percent in 1992," reported political analyst David Wasserman, "an accelerating trend that confirms that America's political fabric, geographically, is tearing apart."

Then there are our neighbors in this increasingly globalized world, some of whom look to this country as a land of opportunity (like my Swedish and German ancestors before them) or sanctuary (as did Mark's Armenian ancestors; see chapter two) and seek to migrate. Such population movements have done much to revitalize denominations such as ours, where first- and second-generation immigrants from Latin America,

Asia, and Africa now worship and serve alongside European Americans like me. But early in his term, President Trump made clear his intention to restrict immigration—even by refugees fleeing brutal violence in countries such as Syria. Evangelical leaders including Leith Anderson, Samuel Rodriguez, and World Vision president Richard Stearns protested that refugee resettlement programs provide "a vital opportunity for our churches to live out the biblical commands to love our neighbors, to make disciples of all nations, and to practice hospitality." Yet Pew found that 76 percent of white evangelicals approved of the president's action—making them twice as likely as other Americans to support a temporary ban on all refugees.

We are literally seeking out neighbors that we love as ourselves—that is, we love them for their resemblance to us. But that's not what Jesus meant. He answers the lawyer's question with the parable of the good Samaritan (Lk 10:30-37), implying that we can't truly love others if we're not willing to cross the boundaries that separate one tribe from another. And while too many Americans are moving too many other Americans from the category of "neighbor" to something more like "enemy," Jesus preached, "You have heard that it was said, 'You shall love your neighbor and hate your enemy.' But I say to you, Love your enemies and pray for those who persecute you" (Mt 5:43-44). "My love," understood Johanna Petersen, "was very deep when I realized that I gained more from [my enemies] than from my best friends."

Can We Still Hope?

For the whole law is summed up in a single commandment, "You shall love your neighbor as yourself." If, however, you bite and devour one another, take care that you are not consumed by one another.

GALATIANS 5:14-15

Time would fail to tell of everything about me that requires repentance and renewal. I hope that at least one paragraph has held up a mirror to your own life, revealing how you too submit to a reign other than God's, seek charity without justice or justice without grace, or live in fear rather than hope. But as I approach the end of this survey, I'm sure you're wishing I'd said more about some particular way that we twenty-first-century Christians are failing to love God and our neighbors as we ought.

On one level, that's inevitable. This is but one chapter in a relatively short book. But I wonder whether it doesn't point to a deeper problem facing Christians today: that we can't even agree on the problems, let alone the solutions.

Jesus prayed that his followers "not belong to the world, just as I do not belong to the world"; instead, they should "be one" as he and his Father are one (Jn 17:14, 21). But the body of Christ often lets itself be shaped by the centrifugal forces of the world, such that even marriage—one of this life's most profound expressions of human unity—tears us apart. While Paul's ancient words still exhort us to "clothe yourselves with love, which binds everything together in perfect harmony" (Col 3:14), we still find it easier to "bite and devour one another" (Gal 5:15).

I fear that we've learned to talk in such a way—not so much *to* as *past* each other—that we don't even mean the same things by the same words. But Scripture reminds us that the Holy Spirit "intercedes with sighs too deep for words" (Rom 8:26). Sighs for love, justice, mercy, and grace that are deeper than how we use those words. Sighs for unity, which itself is of that same Spirit (Eph 4:3).

And so "if we hope for what we do not see"—what we can scarcely name with one voice—we may still "wait for it with patience" (Rom 8:25). If nothing else, to choose the Pietist option is to choose to live in hope.

CHAPTER 2

Hoping for Better Times

Racial injustice, mass incarceration, immigration reform, terrorist threats, war, the refugee crisis, the environment, poverty, differences in perspective on human sexuality, disparities in educational and employment opportunities, fixed political positions, an unwillingness to listen or learn . . . Need I go on? As Chris made clear in the previous chapter, the list of challenges facing the church and our world can be overwhelming. The idea of being hopeful can seem foolish.

Yet to abandon hope would be to imagine ourselves either more challenged or at least more aware than those who have lived in previous times. We are neither. We are people in need of remembering on what and whom our hope relies. This was at the heart of the early Pietists' message: the need to return to the foundation of our hope for the future amid the challenges of our day.

For the believer in the God revealed in Scripture and most supremely in Jesus Christ, that hope has never been rooted in the ever-changing, often challenging circumstances of our world. Rather, it is a hope rooted in a future promised by the God who raised Jesus from the dead. As theologian Kyle Roberts puts it,

> In the resurrection of Jesus, Christians have been newly born "into a living hope" and an irrepressible inheritance (1 Peter 1:3-4). Christian hope is neither an object to possess nor a skill to master; rather, it is a gift that comes through Christ and is sustained by the Spirit. It is animated by the irruption of God's kingdom into this present world of ambiguity, difficulty, and suffering.

The early Pietists proclaimed this confident Christian hope boldly, not in a time of ease, prosperity, and clear-cut solutions but in a time of extreme challenges that historians call the "General Crisis" of the seventeenth century. The first Pietists knew well the trials and troubles that life could bring. Following the Thirty Years' War, Europe had been decimated by war, famine, and disease. What is now Germany had lost as much as a quarter of its population and was divided into hundreds of little fiefdoms, with each local ruler proclaiming himself God's designated representative. To make things worse, Europe was in the throes of the Little Ice Age, with shorter growing seasons weakening an already stagnant economy.

It was understandably a time of fear regarding the future. And it was also the time in which Philipp Spener wrote of how God is the one sure foundation of our hope. Indeed, he insisted that this God-rooted hope is not simply for better times in a far-flung future but for a better future we can begin living into now. "Above all, [Spener] hoped for better times for the church," emphasizes Dale W. Brown in his book *Understanding Pietism*:

> His optimism concerning the immanent power of the Spirit prompted him to regard pristine primitive Christianity as a historical possibility for the future. He attempted to walk a middle road between a utopianism based on the hope for an actual earthly kingdom on the one hand and a despair of any improvement in the world on the other. . . . It was his hope for better times which gave the Protestant church of the second century following the Reformation the conviction that Christianity had been preserved through the struggle of the Thirty Years' War for the purpose of fulfilling a mission to the world. Spener believed that the eschatological hope must become a present reality: the kingdom, which will be completely realized only in the future, must begin to penetrate present history through the renewal of the church, evangelistic endeavors, and various philanthropic and social missions.

While most European Christians were demoralized and anxious about the future, the Pietists were convinced that, as Mordecai had advised Esther in another terrible time of testing, it was precisely "for just such a time as this" (Esther 4:14) that God had given them life and called them to be his people.

Their God-given hope was not an otherworldly one, as is often suggested, imagining a future when God's people would be removed from the suffering and trouble of our world. The Pietists' hope was for the redemption of *this* world. It was, as Jesus taught us to pray, a hope that God's kingdom would come and God's will would be done on earth as it is in heaven (Mt 6:10).

Like Spener and his followers, those choosing the Pietist option today believe that God is answering this prayer and that we, relying on the grace of God, have the privilege of serving as a part of God's answer

> Christ's church has been called together not to invite people to escape the world but to serve on the front line of his kingdom's advance into it.

to it. They are confident that God is engaged in overcoming the devastating realities of sin, death, and evil. They know that the critical turning point in the battle has already been won through the resurrection of Jesus Christ. And they rejoice that Christ's church has been called together not to invite people to escape the world but to serve on the front line of his kingdom's advance into it.

Such hopeful confidence is not a breezy optimism, unaware of how, for all of our God-inspired efforts, we continually fall short of the good we desire to accomplish. As Spener writes in *Pia Desideria*, "We are not living in a Platonic state, and so it is not possible to have everything perfect and according to rule. The evil circumstances of our time are therefore to be borne with compassion rather than bewailed with anger." Nevertheless, he goes on to say, "We are not forbidden to seek perfection, but we are urged on toward it. . . . [Though] I cheerfully concede that here in this life we shall not manage that."

Spener was convinced that progress was possible, despite our inevitable shortcomings, and that better times were within reach for the church and the world we are called to love in Christ's name. This conviction was the basis of the proposals he offered in *Pia Desideria*, proposals that the following chapters will make clear can foster the renewal of the church and revitalize the church's impact for good in our world today.

A Life-Activating Hope

Blessed be the God and Father of our Lord Jesus Christ! By his great mercy he has given us a new birth into a living hope through the resurrection of Jesus Christ from the dead.

1 PETER 1:3

The Pietists taught that we should wait patiently for the fulfillment of our ultimate hope of Christ's return and the reign of God's kingdom becoming a full reality for all. Yet they also taught that we should not wait passively. The nineteenth-century Pietist preacher Christoph Blumhardt urged Christians to engage in "active expectation." As they awaited that future day, their driving shorter-term hope was that the church would move forward in the present day to become all that God intended it to be in this world. Their vision was that the promised power of God would flow in and through his people in such a way that we would live as witnesses to the reality of God's coming kingdom and participate in its advancement in our world.

This sense of "active expectation" is at the heart of the Pietists' hope for the renewal of Christianity. The promised future revealed in the light of Christ's resurrection draws us to increasingly live with it in view by the power of the Holy Spirit. As Michelle Clifton-Soderstrom writes in her book on Pietist ethics, *Angels, Worms, and Bogeys*, the Pietists' hope was both "an excellence, . . . that strength of character that lives patiently in the midst of human sin and brokenness," and "an action . . . the enactment of the content of our faith. Hope is participating in building the earthly kingdom with an eye toward the heavenly. The heavenly kingdom, in other words, is the blueprint from which we build."

Spener and his contemporaries' vision of better times was not just of the joyful day of Christ's return, nor of pleasurable days of ease as they awaited it. Their vision was for the church, empowered by Christ's Spirit, revealing Christ's love to the world. In this they not only looked to the future to discern the kingdom purposes they were called to work toward. They also looked to the past and the early church's example of such kingdom work bearing great fruit in a broken world. That encouragement from the past and their hopeful vision for the future led them to action—positive, faithful, loving action as they sought to live out the legacy entrusted to them and live into the future promised to them by God.

The powerful effect such hope can have on one's character and actions, Clifton-Soderstrom writes, was exemplified by August Hermann Francke. Describing the institutions Francke established in the German city of Halle, she states, "Those who hope build, and build he did. He built orphanages, welcomed the widows and beggars, and effected social change. He reformed schools for children of all classes, included poor girls in his educational innovations, and responded to other social needs, turning Halle into a thriving city of social reform." She concludes, "How should we hope? We hope by having faith that God will bring creation to fruition and by allowing love to work in such a way that we give ourselves over to our neighbors."

It's no coincidence that Francke's hope took concrete form in care for those whom society tended to marginalize. "In the power of the resurrection," observes Kyle Roberts, "Christian hope overcomes the ambiguity and despair caused by the universality of death. In consequence, no practice of care for any segment of society—whether the sick, dying, or mentally ill—seems 'not worth the trouble.'" From the earliest days of the Christian church, living by the light of the resurrection hope has led Jesus' followers to enter boldly into settings and relationships where despair might otherwise make such action seem a waste of time and energy. Indeed, one of the hallmarks of the church at its best through the ages has been its unrelenting commitment to care for those society has deemed unworthy and beyond helping, and its tireless efforts to strive for justice, mercy, and opportunity for those society has pushed to the fringes, neglected, and oppressed.

A better future is one in which God's people are becoming more Christ-like—that is, living lives increasingly aligned with Christ's

> A better future is one in which God's people are becoming more Christ-like—that is, living lives increasingly aligned with Christ's example and teaching.

example and teaching. It is a future in which the great commandments of loving God and loving neighbor, the Great Commission of making disciples of all nations, and the great prayer of Jesus for unity among his followers are being pursued and lived out. As we wait patiently for the second coming of Christ, we aim our prayers, our energies, and our lives expectantly toward better times for the church and our world, times in which God's people are more fully living and loving and serving, as Francke put it, "to God's glory and neighbor's good."

Choosing Hope

Rejoice in hope, be patient in suffering, persevere in prayer.

ROMANS 12:12

When I think about hope, I think of my Armenian maternal grandmother, who lived with us through much of my childhood. I vividly remember the stories she told of her experience in the genocide perpetrated by the Ottoman government against Armenians during World War I. It was horrific. More than one million Armenians lost their lives, including most of my grandparents' family members. Their property, homes, and even entire villages were taken away.

My grandmother started her journey through that terrible time with six children; two died before her very eyes, two were taken from her and she never saw them again, and two finally made it with her to the United States. The agony of the challenges she and others faced is almost beyond description: the choice of whether to let her children go with Turkish soldiers who promised to feed them when she had nothing to offer them herself. The question raised by a woman struggling to cross a river with Grandmother's son in one arm and a blanket in the other. It's ridiculous to anyone in retrospect and to my grandmother at the time, but the woman asked in all sincerity which one she should drop and leave behind.

Grandma finally made her way to the United States with only two remaining children—only to watch one die soon afterward. Far too many horrific, heart-wrenching stories arose from the experience, but for the most part she stuck to telling those that offered glimpses of good along the way. She shared stories of good and kind Turkish neighbors who helped her at the beginning of her journey. She spoke of the Turkish soldier, a Muslim, who showed her their shared humanity, calling her "Mama" as he led her like an angel sent from God to reconnect with her children when they'd become separated in the city of Aleppo. She spoke of Christian missionaries who helped her and her surviving children finally make it to the United States. She told of the letter those missionaries had written, one she was never able to read and never saw again, that she handed to the immigration officers as they were turning her away at the US border, a letter that somehow convinced the officers to let her and her children in.

All of these stories served as testimonies to me of the light that can be seen shining amid the darkness. More than that, they have served as words of encouragement as I seek to be the kind of person who serves others, like those who offered support to my family members, especially when it is most difficult and even dangerous to do so. Most of all, her stories and her life have been a testimony to me of what it means to keep venturing forward with hope in Christ come what may.

I'm told that my grandmother's favorite psalm was Psalm 22, the one Jesus quoted on the cross. "My God, my God, why have you forsaken me?" the psalmist cried (Ps 22:1), as did Jesus in his time of deepest pain (Mk 15:34). Reflecting on the psalm in an email, my sister Susan Pattie writes:

> When you read it, it is easy to imagine why [it was grandma's favorite]. We remember Grandma singing "Heavenly Sunshine" and other songs of grace and joy—and goodness. But during that period, she was feeling abandoned, as everyone must have felt—but at the same time affirming her faith and believing that God

would somehow take care of her and her family, even in death. There is a fine line between giving up and accepting that indeed death is a real possibility though you are going to fight as hard as you can—with God's help.

I've been aware as long as I can remember that others came through the experience with very different perspectives. Some became atheists, unable to imagine the possibility that there could be a God, to say nothing of a good God, in a world of such evil. It is an understandable conclusion, but my grandmother made it clear that it wasn't the only one. In fact, her stories, her witness, and her whole life served as a testimony that faith and hope not only were possible but enabled one to both notice and boldly participate in God's loving activity in the midst of our broken world.

This decision to put one's faith in God and so to allow hope in the fulfillment of God's promises to blossom and bear the fruit of love is at the heart of the Pietist option. The Pietists were convinced that this decision needed to be made intentionally and personally by each person. Baptism is not sufficient. Being born in the right country or to the right family is not enough. Going to church, participating in the sacraments, and reading the Bible are not adequate by themselves. *Faith* is necessary. A living faith out of which hope springs up, inspiring love, directing life, and reshaping the world.

This was a crucial and frequent distinction made by the German Pietists, as Chris pointed out in the previous chapter. They spoke often of the contrast between "living faith" and "dead orthodoxy." The latter, they were convinced, can have all the right answers to biblical and theological questions, or at least blithely imagine it so, yet miss out entirely on a living faith in the living God revealed to us in Jesus Christ. The Pietists' call to faith went far beyond simply agreeing to an abstract set of beliefs or giving assent to some vague idea of a greater spiritual power. The call was to a decision to place one's faith and hope firmly in God, who alone can forgive, free, empower, and ultimately protect and provide for us as we seek to live the life we've been created to live.

Such a living faith is not something we can fabricate for ourselves or force on others. It is a gift, a grace, that can come only "from above"

(Jn 3:7). Yet the Pietists were clear that, even so, it is a gift that must be received and taken to heart. And while our inclination or ability to do so will, no doubt, be influenced by the circumstances and experiences of our lives, each of us must make that choice—and that choice makes all the difference.

This volitional element to the life of faith is a consistent characteristic of the wide swath of Christianity influenced by Pietism, including the Great Awakenings and many evangelical renewal movements since. Arising at a time when the particular place you lived determined your religious affiliation, the call to a personal decision about what you believe or whether you believe at all was significant, and it remains so to our day. This focus on individual choice has remained of paramount importance throughout the evangelical church and beyond. Unfortunately, however, many have fallen into the mistaken notion that the choice only needs to be made once.

"Blessed Are Those Who Trust in the Lord"

Don't misunderstand. We are not arguing here about whether God's grace is sufficient. Having put our faith in God's grace, we can trust "that the one who began a good work among you will bring it to completion by the day of Jesus Christ" (Phil 1:6). On a practical level, though, our part is to decide again and again, day after day, whether to trust God's faithfulness. Choosing to trust God is a recurrent necessity for us, as it was for Abraham and Sarah and everyone who has walked by faith since. Each

> Choosing to trust God is a recurrent necessity for us.

and every day, we must choose whether to trust God and thereby to "be strong and courageous" (Josh 1:9), setting out to live according to his Word and call in our lives.

For many of us this continual necessity of choosing to live by faith is the great disconnect. Faith does not always come easily to most of us. Like Jacob, we find ourselves wrestling with God amid the challenges of life (Gen 32:22-32). Like the Hebrew people in the book of Judges, we find ourselves anxious for our economic, social, and physical well-being and tempted to place our faith in the impotent idols of our day rather than the faithful God of the ages. As polls like the June 2016 Pew survey noted in chapter one point out, despite saying we've put our faith in God, Christians frequently look every bit as fearful as the next person while we watch the news, speak to our neighbors, listen to (or more likely, tune out) alternate points of view, walk into a voting booth, and go about our lives.

As the Hebrew people yet again faced economic, social, and physical upheaval in the Babylonian exile, God declared:

> Cursed are those who trust in mere mortals
>   and make mere flesh their strength,
>   whose hearts turn away from the LORD.
> They shall be like a shrub in the desert,
>   and shall not see when relief comes.
> They shall live in the parched places of the wilderness,
>   in an uninhabited salt land.
>
> Blessed are those who trust in the LORD,
>   whose trust is the LORD.
> They shall be like a tree planted by water,
>   sending out its roots by the stream.
> It shall not fear when heat comes,
>   and its leaves shall stay green;
> in the year of drought it is not anxious,
>   and it does not cease to bear fruit. (Jer 17:5-8)

We too are tempted through sometimes terrifying challenges to abandon our faith in God and rest in the fickle, fleeting powers and inadequate idols of our world. So Jeremiah's word is one we need to hear and heed, again and again. It is more than a call to place our faith in God as a one-time act. Rather, it is an exhortation to continually root ourselves in the grace of God through faith and persevere in allowing our aspirations and actions to be inspired by God's promises through hope. It is an invitation to join with God and others in eagerly serving toward the future in which God's promises are completely fulfilled and the experience of God's love is the reality for all.

This is the bottom-line, foundational decision we need to make. Pietism reminds Christians who imagine themselves to be people of faith to actually *be* people of faith, to put our hope resolutely in God and live like it. As we choose to hope, the fruit will become evident.

PART TWO

Proposals for Renewal

CHAPTER 3

A More Extensive Listening
to the Word of God

From the beginning, Pietism has been a practical program for renewal. Spener didn't just hold out hope that the problems he named could be solved. His Pietist option included six specific suggestions for working toward making that hope a reality, suggestions we're going to adapt to the needs of the twenty-first century. The first two proposals called Protestants back to key themes of the Reformation: the centrality of Scripture, and what clergy and laity had in common as "priests." Then Spener addressed two of the problems exacerbated by the Reformation: a temptation to make too much of right belief and too little of right action, and the disunity of a church splintered into bickering churches. Finally, Spener offered his take on two perpetual needs: the ongoing formation of people who seek not only to follow Christ but to become more Christ-like, and the proclamation of the gospel in a way that reaches the hearts and minds of all people.

In this chapter we will look at the first of those suggestions, the one Spener said was "the powerful means" by which we can "bring about faith and its fruits." In his book *Pia Desideria* he wrote, "We know that by nature we have no good in us. If there is to be any good in us, it must be brought about by God. *To this end the Word of God is the powerful means.*"

Of course, in our day many of us are far from convinced "that by nature we have no good in us." We tend to be far more inclined to imagine we are fundamentally good and just need to try a little harder, or that the spiritual spark we need is actually hidden deep inside us and all we really have to do is get in touch with our better, more beautiful selves buried within.

In sharp contrast, Spener followed Martin Luther in arguing that we cannot achieve the good we long for apart from the grace of God. Spener would no doubt acknowledge that all are created in the image of God and thereby worthy of dignity, respect, and love, but he was quite clear that we cannot accomplish the good we desire and need apart from the gracious intervention of God. As the apostle Paul admitted, "I know that nothing good dwells within me, that is, in my flesh. I can will what is right, but I cannot do it" (Rom 7:18). If we are to hope for a better future on earth as well as in the world to come, we truly and profoundly need God's help. And thankfully, God offers that help. For Spener was right: "The more at home the Word of God is among us, the more we shall bring about faith and its fruits."

An Altar Where We Meet the Living God

But isn't God's Word already very much at home among us? *The Guinness Book of World Records* declares year after year that the Bible is the world's best-selling book; it is everywhere available and accessible. Over five billion copies have been printed in hundreds of languages, and millions of people go online to read Scripture via websites and apps such as Bible Gateway.

Though it is everywhere present to us, many Christians are slow to present ourselves fully to the Scriptures' powerful influence. Though the Bible is all *around* us, we are often slow to invite it to be alive *within* us. We are too often reluctant or too preoccupied to welcome God's Word into our hearts and minds to nourish and transform us, to teach, reprove, correct, and train us in the God-designed, God-inspired way of life (2 Tim 3:16-17). "This much is certain," Spener wrote confidently,

> the diligent use of the Word of God, which consists not only of listening to sermons but also of reading, meditating, and dis-cussion (Ps. 1:2), must be the chief means for reforming something. . . . The Word of God remains the seed from which all that is good in us must grow. If we succeed in getting the people to seek eagerly and diligently in the book of life for their joy, their spiritual life

will be wonderfully strengthened and they will become altogether different people.

Getting "people to seek eagerly and diligently in the book of life for their joy" was a foundational principle for the German Pietists as they sought the spiritual renewal of individual believers, local congregations, and the church as a whole. In this Spener and other Pietists were simply following through on a key proposition of the Reformation, one its leaders had taught and worked toward, yet backed off from. When Reformers such as Luther realized that encouraging the general populace to read, interpret, and apply the Scriptures provoked challenges to the current order of society, they became alarmed and argued for a more hierarchically controlled communication of the Word of God. By Spener's

> Though the Bible is all *around* us, we are often slow to invite it to be alive *within* us.

time, the teachings of the various churches expressed in their confessions and creeds were generally understood to have equal authority to the Scriptures. The Bible's purpose had become primarily to support what was already believed and understood or, at best, to use in arguments about how best to articulate such things. The idea of the Scriptures having transformative power had long since been left behind.

In sharp contrast, Pietists understood the Bible to be "an altar where one meets the living God." Far from simply being a receptacle for information—even God-inspired information—the Pietists held that the Scriptures are primarily a God-inspired gift for transformation. They taught that when we reverently approach the Bible, inviting the Holy Spirit to open our minds and hearts and lives to the Word of God, the Scriptures are the powerful means by which God can equip us to live out the good we were created to accomplish. They have the power to transform us by the renewal of our minds, as the apostle Paul urges, so that we will not be conformed to this world but rather able to discern and, by God's grace, do the will of God (Rom 12:2).

Transformation, not just some minor adjustments to our lives and world, is what we need. And this is what is offered every time we come to the Scriptures: a transformation that leads us to live, as the Pietists often put it, in such a way that we bring glory to God and good to our neighbor. As we come to the Scriptures with a humble, repentant, willing spirit, God is able by the power at work within us "to accomplish abundantly far more than all we can ask or imagine" (Eph 3:20).

This eager, expectant attitude in approaching the Bible is too frequently missing today despite the Bible's status as a bestseller. Kenneth A. Briggs, a veteran religion reporter and author of *The Invisible Bestseller: Searching for the Bible in America*, finds that

> we still love [the Bible] to some extent as an artifact, as a keepsake, as a gift to people we think do read the Bible even though we may not, so it remains very popular that way and something almost like—I don't want to say quite "rabbit's foot," but it's sort of like that. Every home should have at least one, and the average is between four and five.

Even when the Bible is studied, Briggs argues, we tend to treat it as "either rote learning or what they used to call the 'banking system of education,' where the banker hands out stuff and everybody takes it and leaves." Our focus in approaching the Scriptures is, at best, on increasing our knowledge rather than on transformation or, as Spener puts it, becoming "altogether different people."

This emphasis on transformation is not to set up a false dichotomy between studying the Bible to increase our knowledge and doing so to invite transformation. It is to say that one without the other is a spiritual dead end. Our modern interest in understanding the context of the biblical authors and the circumstances in which they wrote is directly linked to the influence of the early Pietists. They wanted to know everything they could about who wrote the biblical books and why, what their circumstances were, and how a given passage fit within the biblical and historical context. But they wanted this knowledge so as to give greater opportunity for the Holy Spirit to speak through the Word in a fresh and personal way in their current context. Simply acquiring greater amounts of biblical information can lead to inflated egos rather than spiritual maturity. Conversely, asking God to transform us without actually looking to God's teaching in the Scriptures is just another route toward doing whatever seems right in our own eyes.

Attentiveness to the Scriptures

Do not seek to measure and arrange Scripture according to your mind and understanding, but rather determine your understanding according to Scripture.

AUGUST HERMANN FRANCKE

What we need, as Spener proposed in 1675, is "a more extensive use of the Word of God among us." We need a broader and deeper reading of, listening to, and attentiveness to the Scriptures.

To be clear, the primary problem is not that society at large isn't paying enough attention to the Word of God, despite the frequently heard complaint regarding the decreasing presence of Scripture in the public sphere (in schools, on the walls of courtrooms, etc.). The far greater and more troubling issue is that too few churches and too few of us who call ourselves followers of Christ are listening attentively to God's Word. According to Briggs,

> Most of our history has been a rather Bible-less Christianity that was dictated or defined mostly by the hierarchical church, not by people who read the Bible. . . . We gained the freedom to approach it, and then in the current age, we have ceded that exploration to media, to entertainment forms, to prepackaged interpretations that are delivered in video, audio and pulpit forms so that there's a substitute Bible that isn't the Bible, per se, at the same time that people aren't reading.

We have the chance, more than ever before, to read and study the Bible and thus to be nourished and changed by God. Yet even with such an historic opportunity, we choose to allow others to filter, frame, interpret, and apply it for us. We aren't coming to the altar ourselves to listen to, be shaped by, and be led by God. We are outsourcing this life-critical work, as we do with so many things in our society—except that in this case, we are outsourcing our eating of the spiritual nourishment we need.

"The spiritual power of the pietist movement lay in its recovery of a vital and dynamic use of the Bible," wrote the authors of our denomination's 1963 paper "Biblical Authority and Christian Freedom," to which they added the line quoted above: "To read it properly, therefore, is to find it an altar where one meets the living God and receives personally the reality of redemption." As we come to the Scriptures, God leads us to repentance and enables our reformation. This gift that God offers is not simply the one-time experience of conversion but an ongoing process of sanctification, of progressive spiritual development as God shapes us increasingly toward his good purpose—and through us, our institutions and even society.

Going Back to the Center

As Luther and other Reformers became acutely aware, opening the door to the challenges that come with change can be frightening, threatening to the status quo, even dangerous. Alternately, though, closing the door to what we currently consider heretical thought can also close the door on allowing the Holy Spirit to speak to and lead us in fresh and unanticipated ways. As the wise authors of "Biblical Authority and Christian Freedom" put it over fifty years ago:

> Christian vitality has not always been maintained by the majority. It has, in fact, often been found only in small minorities. Such minorities have no voice where conformity to "official" interpretations is required. Unless we wish to stifle all emergent spiritual vitality, we must be sure that people within our fellowship will be free to express themselves in ways which are different from the majority position without the fear of being labeled as disloyal.

This is a challenge, God knows—and we do too. As a church leader myself, I am aware that for a community to be healthy, there have to be some boundaries placed around behavior. I'm aware that not every idea is as good as the next and that some are downright misleading and dangerous. Yet at the same time I'm aware that our tendency as human beings is to react to the pendulum swinging too far to one side by swinging it too far in the other direction. It's easy for us to react emotionally, trying to combat or quash perceived excesses by going instead to another extreme. But more often than not, this simply leads to further reactivity. It almost never facilitates deeper community, greater communication, more mature relationships, and the kind of unity Jesus prayed would be the church's greatest witness to the world.

We need to be wary of this polarizing tendency of so many who honestly strive to be right but somehow end up being far from a part of God's answer to Jesus' fervent prayer for unity among his followers. In contrast, the Pietist option is to seek and focus on the common ground on which we can stand—to trust that we're better together than apart. It acknowledges that there may be times at which, in our human limitations, we are not able to remain united. Yet if and when such division becomes our reality, we humbly confess that it represents a failure in our faithfulness to Christ's call, in our witness to the world, and likely in our imagination in finding a way forward together.

A driving impulse of the Pietist option is the prayer for a greater, more faithful, God-inspired imagination in finding our way forward *together* in Christ. As we write this book in the year of the Reformation's five hundredth anniversary, many are celebrating the great good that arose through that movement. Yet our joy is tempered by our lament over the bitter divisions that emerged, the extent to which dividing into factions has become commonplace among us, and the degree to which we are known more by our manifold divisions than by our love for one another and our neighbors in the world. I for one have often wished that Christ's followers of that time had been able to discover another way forward besides splitting between the Roman Catholic Church and various Protestant denominations. More significantly, I long for those of us seeking to follow Christ now to learn from our forebears' experience and prayerfully seek a different path, choose a different option, amid our differences in perspective today. It is a difficult choice, of course, full of myriad challenges. Yet our call is to be a part of the answer to Jesus' prayer.

The Pietist option means walking an uncharted path by faith, venturing in what is increasingly a countercultural direction. It means resisting both our inner inclination to go our own ways and the ever-more-sophisticated voices of marketers, politicians, and activists who would separate us out into flocks of our world's making. It means centering our identities and our lives in Christ above all as we lean toward and support one another on this difficult journey, humbly listening to and learning from each other as we go.

We are better together than apart, even though being united is often hard work and may frequently seem impossible. We need to claim our common ground together in the Scriptures, leaving room for challenges to our perspectives, remembering that all of us come to the Scriptures, as to all of life, shaped by our experiences and needs. None of us sees or hears everything. We filter what we take in so as to not be overwhelmed by it. We focus on certain things and not on others, fitting what we see and hear into preconceived patterns to make sense of all the information before us. We must resolutely come together in humility before the Scriptures to listen and respond more faithfully to the Word of God.

It reminds me of playing racquetball against a formidable opponent. I was fast, full of energy, and committed, hitting the ball just right every chance I got. He just stood his ground in the middle of the court and kept me running. It didn't matter how often I got my shot right; I was out of position. I wasn't centered. I wasn't standing in the one place from which I could possibly win the game. My only chance was to reclaim the center of the court and establish myself there.

We've given up the center. We're chasing after the ball wherever our society tells us we need to focus our attention. We've allowed the ever-changing and always divisive issues of the day to become the ground on which we stake our claim. We often refuse to humbly cede points, admitting that we just don't know it all. In our pride, we stray far from the only place from which our victory can ever be gained. We need to come back to Jesus, take our stand with him in the gracious love of God, seeking him as he is revealed to us in the Scriptures and receiving the reality of redemption as we encounter him at the altar where we meet the living God.

Biblical interpretations, theological precision, political acumen, and even good deeds (important as these and other things are) cannot serve as the center ground out of which our identity, our fellowship with one another, or our hope arise. We must stand together in the grace of God, to which we have obtained access through our Lord Jesus Christ (Rom 5:1-11). There, as the apostle Paul makes clear, we can "boast in our hope of sharing the glory of God." This grace we are offered is free and freeing, and it's also costly. It's not just a free ride to continue on our merry way without truly needing repentance. Real engagement with grace will bring us back to Scripture precisely because we want to follow—and encourage one another to follow—this gracious Jesus. There, standing in the grace of God, we can and must wrestle with our differences while remaining together on common ground.

Trusting in that grace, we can approach both the Scriptures and one another in humility and hope, seeking God's presence, power, and leading together. Trusting in that grace, we can honestly admit our differences of interpretations and applications and in love wrestle with them together. Trusting in that grace, the Pietist option is one that calls us forever back to the Bible, submitting ourselves, our interpretations, and our decisions again and again to God. For the early Pietists trusting God's grace, no matter how settled a particular issue seemed to be, the question, Where is it written? was always appropriate and invited. Trusting in God's grace, we can generously extend to one another the grace God has extended to us and, as a community of grace that is admittedly far more diverse and challenging than we'd sometimes prefer, make our way forward as sisters and brothers together.

Far from living as a community whose greatest witness is our love for one another, we are often unwilling to even worship, pray, and especially read the Scriptures with people we disagree with on particular theological or social issues. Many of us avoid humbly submitting ourselves to the possibility of a perspective-changing engagement with the Scriptures as we seek God's Word together. Such humility is an essential ingredient of the Pietist ethos and of our fervent hope for better times ahead for Christ's incredibly diverse, far too divided church. At the heart of this humility is the willingness and indeed commitment to come continually before the Word of God with a repentant, eager, teachable spirit.

We need to come to the altar where we meet the living God, opening our hearts and minds to the Word of God and inviting God to speak in fresh ways into our lives, church, and world. As Briggs told an interviewer, "One thing we miss in [not reading the Bible] is the potential to enlarge our minds and hearts and spirits. I think the Bible is the springboard to opening all kinds of ideas, thoughts, beliefs about what our life is about. And I think without it, it narrows our perspective and gives us a much more truncated view of what the possibilities are." We need an inspired imagination, a greater voice to speak into the worn-out boxes of our ways of thinking and break us free to pursue possibilities beyond what we've convinced ourselves we are capable of.

Listening Attentively to God's Word

Exegetically, Spener and Francke differed from their contemporaries not only in their view of Scripture as the supreme authority in the church but also in their stress on the practical purposes and goals of Bible study. . . . Pietists believed the Bible had been communicated to man in order to edify, console, encourage, warn, reprimand, and help the church and its members as well as to lead men and women to God by bringing about repentance and change. For Pietists the Bible became a devotional resource more than a source of doctrine, a guide to life rather than just the source of belief and faith.

DALE W. BROWN

So how does a Pietist go about coming to this altar to meet the living God? One simple way of thinking about it for me has been the acronym PRAY.

P—Pray. Pietists are known for pursuing a personal, life-undergirding devotional life that shapes who we are and all we do. This ongoing, conversational walk with God isn't limited to when we read the Scriptures, but it certainly happens there. In many ways it begins there. We Pietists come to the Bible in prayer, submitting ourselves to God, inviting the Holy Spirit to enlighten us, asking God to speak to us and enable us to live according to God's gracious purpose. We pray as we begin, as we read, as we conclude, and as we go. We pray.

In a guide for reading the Scriptures, Spener wrote, "The first means to proper Bible reading is heartfelt prayer." And he emphasized that it wasn't just a matter of offering a perfunctory prayer as we start. "We are to close off our reading with prayer so that the Holy Spirit might also hallow what we have read and seal it in us that not only do we hold the Word in our thoughts but that the Spirit's power might impress itself into our soul and that we might hold the Word in a good heart and bring forth fruit in patience (Luke 8:15)." Our reading of the Bible can never be reduced to a simple human endeavor, something we try to do in our own wisdom and power. As Luther wrote, "Where the Spirit does not open the Scripture, the Scripture is not understood even though it is read."

When we pray, trusting in the power of the Holy Spirit, our encounter with the Scriptures is always far more than just an academic or intellectual exercise. Though deeply committed to engaging our intellect in the encounter, we read the Scriptures with prayerful anticipation and expectation of something far more. We come to the Bible presenting ourselves "as a living sacrifice," praying that we would not be conformed to this world but transformed by the renewal of our minds (Rom 12:1-2), that by God's grace we might truly love God, love one another, and love our neighbor. This, of course, is what the teaching of all the Scriptures— the Law, the Prophets, and Jesus himself—points to and is summed up by (Mt 22:36-40).

R—Repent. "Repent, for the kingdom of heaven has come near," Jesus preached as he began his ministry (Mt 3:2; 4:17), and it is forever the right attitude when we come near to God. An essential lesson of the spiritual life is that God is always near; therefore an attitude of humble willingness in turning toward God and seeking God's leading is always appropriate. Nevertheless, as we approach the Scriptures as "an altar where one meets the living God," it is especially critical that we are intentional about having an attitude of repentance. We come to the Scriptures not to check a box in our to-do list or to attain mastery over the words but to open ourselves to God's to-do list for, in, and through us as we surrender ourselves to God's mastery over us.

When I think of a repentant spirit, I think of the younger and older sons of the loving father in Jesus' parable in Luke 15. The younger, who has wandered so far and squandered so much, repents. That is, he turns and reorients his life toward his father. This prodigal has no sense of entitlement, no grand expectations as to what his father will do for him. He only knows that his hope for the future lies in the direction of his father's care. And as soon as he turns in that direction, while he is still a long way from home, his father runs to embrace him, love him, and welcome him home.

The older brother, in contrast, never quite allows himself to be so loved, at least not as Luke's retelling of the story comes to an end. In his own ways, though always in close physical proximity to his father, in his own pride, insecurity, and busyness, he has never simply trusted his father's love, received it, and enjoyed it. In his own imagination he has perceived strings to be attached to his father's love. No such restrictions had ever existed in reality. Yet even when he's told otherwise at the close of the parable, it isn't clear whether this beloved son will finally believe in and surrender to such extravagant love. He, like his younger brother, like all of us, desperately needs to turn toward home with his father and believe the good news. As the story ends, his father is still pleading with him, as our heavenly Father does with each of us, inviting him to turn and come back home, to turn and allow himself and his brother both to be loved.

> This is what it means to repent: to turn toward God and let God love us, guide us, and have his way with us.

This is what it means to repent: to turn toward God and let God love us, guide us, and have his way with us. We can't know where it will all lead, what he will do or demand of us. But we know that our hope for the future lies in that direction. We must come to the Scriptures, open ourselves in humility, and trust our Father's love for us as we meet him at the altar of his holy Word. The words of the Pietist hymnodist Lina Sandell express the attitude well: "Now before you, Lord, we gather to receive your precious Word; / let your grace in show'rs, O Father, on our parched hearts be poured. / Send your Holy Spirit o'er us, with your quick'ning fire restore us, / at your table spread before us fill our hung'ring souls, dear Lord."

As children prone to squander the opportunities and resources we are given, we come to the Scriptures to receive the precious Word of our loving Father, who graciously welcomes us. We come as sheep, prone to wander and lose our way, looking again to the Good Shepherd who rejoices to lead us in his right paths. We come back to Jesus, to the Word of God revealed in the Scriptures, and present ourselves as a living sacrifice (Rom 12:1), not simply to add to our knowledge or to be adjusted and tweaked, but to listen and allow ourselves to be loved and transformed to live according to God's gracious will.

A—Ask. Third, ask. Ask questions. Come to the Scriptures asking questions of God and of yourself. Be curious, expectant, imaginative, open, and interested in seeing what you haven't yet seen, understanding what you haven't yet understood, and appreciating what you haven't yet appreciated. Be honest with yourself and with God about what you are feeling, wondering about, and wrestling with. Ask God to help you sort through it all.

Ask others. Ask for help. Ask others to read the Scriptures with you. Ask others to help you listen to the Scriptures, understand them, wrestle with them, and live them. Don't try to listen to God solely on your own. Certainly we should spend time in the Scriptures alone, but we must never imagine that we've got such a direct line to God that we don't need the assistance of others as we seek to listen to God's Word.

Remarkably, one of the key innovations of the Pietist movement was the widespread encouragement of small groups, or conventicles, in which people gathered for Bible study, prayer, discussion, singing, and fellowship. It may well be that these conventicles served as the critical ingredient in enabling the Pietist movement to sweep across Europe and beyond, changing lives and communities along the way. It is a great gift to join with others for accountability and encouragement, as well as for help in listening to, wrestling with, and interpreting what God is saying. Ask others to join you in coming to the altar to meet the living God.

Ask about the whole of the Scriptures. Reflecting on the verse "All scripture is inspired by God and is useful for teaching, for reproof, for correction, and for training in righteousness" (2 Tim 3:16), Spener wrote in *Pia Desideria*, "Accordingly *all* Scripture, without exception, should be known by the congregation if all are to receive the necessary benefit." Our tendency today is too often to read the Bible in bits and pieces, often our favorite bits and pieces repeatedly. In our churches, small groups, and personal devotional times, we need to avail ourselves of the whole of Scripture, even those parts we aren't as enthusiastic about or understanding of, if we are to "receive the necessary benefit."

Ask how any particular passage or verse you are reading fits in with the rest. Ask about the context of what you are reading: about the authors, their situations, their influences, their intentions. Seek the perspectives and insights of others, including those who come from different backgrounds and experiences. Seek deeper understanding by reading commentaries and books and by listening to those who have given themselves to further training and research.

The Covenant Church's resource paper on reading the Bible states, "Belief in the Bible's power and authority to transform us does not mean that understanding happens automatically. All our intellectual capacities are brought to the task of interpretation, and we make use of available information and scholarly tools to bridge the gap between the ancient text and our own lives." It is far too easy and tempting to allow our own experiences and biases to blind us to the very insights and challenges we most need to hear. We need to bring with us the best of our own scholarship, as well as that of the full breadth of the Christian community, as we meet with God and listen to God's Word.

Y—Yes. Finally, read with the word *yes* on the tip of your tongue. Come with a willing spirit and a desire to live fully into the life to which God is calling you. Read with a sense of expectation that God will speak to you and with the intention of being obedient, a hearer *and* a doer of God's Word (Jas 1:22). Don't open the Bible to simply go through the motions. Don't listen to a sermon or engage in a small group simply for entertainment or to sit back with a critical spirit. Don't memorize or meditate on Scripture just to feel better about yourself or to get others or even God to think more highly of you.

Come to the Scriptures to say yes to God. Yes, I want to allow you to love me. Yes, I want to receive the nourishment, guidance, transformation, and empowerment you offer. Yes, I want to love you with all of my heart, soul, mind, and strength, and love my neighbor as myself. Yes, I want your will to be done in and through me. The purpose of studying the Bible is that we would grow to live according to it and thereby to the glory of God.

> **Come to the Scriptures to say yes to God.**

This has always been the opportunity and the test of faith: to walk or not walk according to the gracious Word of God. As the first psalm and so many other passages in Scripture make clear, there are two paths set before us, each day and moment of our lives:

> Blessed is the one
>   who does not walk in step with the wicked
> or stand in the way that sinners take
>   or sit in the company of mockers,
> but whose delight is in the law of the LORD. (Ps 1:1-2 NIV)

We are given the choice of which path we will say yes to. As we come to the Scriptures, we come to meditate on God's Word, to listen to and internalize it, so that we may say yes and so "be careful to act in accordance with all that is written in it. For then you shall make your way prosperous, and then you shall be successful" (Josh 1:8). Then we shall grow into and live out God's gracious purpose "like trees planted by streams of water" (Ps 1:3), yielding good fruit to the glory of God and the good of our neighbor. Practicing this "yes" to the Word of God is at the core of the Pietist option.

Conclusion

We are convinced, as were the Pietists of Spener's time and later eras, that a more extensive, attentive listening to the Word of God is a crucial first step as we seek a more hopeful future for the church, for those of us called by Christ to be members of it, and for the world we are called to love in his name. To quote the paper "Biblical Authority and Christian Freedom" once more:

> If, as individual Christians and as a Christian community, we learn to listen to God's voice breaking through to us day after day, and week by week from the pages of His chosen Book, we will discover a deepening of our love for Him who saves us, a widening of our love for this sinful world, a strengthening of the bonds of fellowship and mutual trust within the Christian community and a growing Christlikeness in the lives of His saints.

We must reclaim our center together in the Scriptures, humbly and purposefully coming back to Jesus there. We come not as if to a simple rule book, focused on our disagreements, pointing fingers at each other, and dividing ourselves by important but less-than-essential aspects of faith, doctrine, and practice. We come as to an altar, before which we humbly seek God's presence, power, and Word with great faith, hope, and love.

CHAPTER 4

The Common Priesthood
for the Common Good

As Mark explained in the preceding chapter, Pietists have always treasured the Bible—but with the intention of being "doers of the word, and not merely hearers who deceive themselves" (Jas 1:22). That was true, for example, of a small group that met in the Swedish province of Värmland in the middle of the nineteenth century. In the lovely description by Glen Wiberg, these Pietists "gathered . . . around the gospel and made the remarkable discovery that because of grace they were also bound to the needs of neighbor." They pooled their scarce funds to buy the freedom of boys and girls forced to work off their parents' debts as farmhands and servants. Like A. H. Francke in the previous century, they founded a school and children's home. Coming back to Jesus, the living Word, through the written word of Scripture taught the members of this conventicle "to care for orphans and widows in their distress, and to keep [themselves] unstained by the world" (Jas 1:27).

But what's most remarkable is that the leader of this project to care for children in distress was herself a widow, with six kids of her own: Maria Nilsdotter, who was called Mor i Vall ("Mother at Vall Farm"). Better than most, she and the other women in her group knew that reading God's Word kept them from conforming to the world by prompting them to care for those society neglected. At Maria's funeral in 1870, her son C. J. Nyvall, an early Covenant evangelist, preached from the Gospel of Matthew: "Whoever welcomes one such child in my name welcomes me" (Mt 18:5).

"There is probably nothing in which historians have been more unfair to Pietism," observes Brethren scholar Dale Brown, "than in defining the mission of the church to society." For example, Mennonite historian Robert Friedmann dismissed Pietism as "a quiet conventicle-Christianity which is primarily concerned with the inner experience of salvation." But Brown insists that

> the Pietist milieu resulted in a desire to transform the living conditions of the poor and oppressed, reform the prison system, abolish slavery, break down rigid class distinctions, establish a more democratic polity, initiate educational reforms, establish philanthropic institutions, increase missionary activity, obtain religious liberty, and propose programs for social justice.

Spener's pious wish for a greater attentiveness to Scripture led Pietists such as Mor i Vall to combine inner devotion with external action.

The fact that this desire for personal and social change was worked out by women on the margins of their society points to the enduring influence of Spener's second proposal: *the establishment and diligent exercise of the spiritual priesthood. . . .* Peter was not addressing preachers alone when he wrote, 'You are a chosen race, a royal priesthood, a holy nation, God's own people, that you may declare the wonderful deeds of him who called you out of darkness into his marvelous light' [1 Pet 2:9]."

How would Pietists define the "the mission of the church to society"? I would sum it up as *the common priesthood seeking the common good.*

The Common (or Spiritual) Priesthood (of All Believers)

Let everyone, therefore, who knows himself to be a Christian, be assured of this, that we are all equally priests.

MARTIN LUTHER

While priests are familiar figures in Roman Catholic, Eastern Orthodox, and Anglican churches, most Protestants (including most Pietists) aren't accustomed to thinking of themselves in such terms. But following Martin Luther, Spener wrote enthusiastically about a priesthood shared by "all

Christians without distinction (1 Pet. 2:9), old and young, male and female, bond and free (Gal. 3:28)." ("In Christ," he reiterated, "the difference between man and woman, in regard to what is spiritual, is abolished.")

You might have heard it described as a *priesthood of all believers*— which is fine, so long as we don't make an extensive doctrinal test the standard for belief or treat doubt as the enemy of faith. Spener and other Pietists also spoke of it as a *spiritual priesthood*—which is fine, so long as we don't think it's detached from the physical needs of this world and all who live in it. But the leading scholar on this topic, Jonathan Strom, prefers *common priesthood* to describe Luther's and Spener's under-standing of the relationship between clergy and laity. That's good enough for me. And I also like that *common* is a synonym for both *shared* and *ordinary*, since much of the important work that we do together as the church is far from flashy.

But rather than getting bogged down with the adjective, let's first make sure we're on the same page about the noun. What does it mean that the people of the church make up a priesthood? What do such priests do?

Increasingly dissatisfied with the hierarchical church of the late Middle Ages, Luther found new wisdom from an old source: the letter to the Hebrews, whose author addressed himself to "holy partners in a heavenly calling" (Heb 3:1). In short, priests are all those who may come into the presence of God, who "approach the throne of grace with boldness, so that we may receive mercy and find grace to help in time of need" (Heb 4:16). We can do this because of Jesus, the Son who "is the reflection of God's glory and the exact imprint of God's very being" (Heb 1:3), who "offered for all time a single sacrifice for sins" (Heb 10:12) and thereby gave his followers "confidence to enter the sanctuary" (Heb 10:19). All those who come back to Jesus—from pastors and professors to widows and the poor—become priests under a high priest who is able "to sympathize with our weaknesses, . . . who in every respect has been tested as we are, yet without sin" (Heb 4:15).

For Spener, priesthood entailed three specific duties, which he ex-plained in more depth in a 1677 pamphlet. First, priests are called to *sacrifice* "themselves with all that they are, so that they may no longer desire to serve themselves, but him who has bought and redeemed them."

Second, to be a priest is to *pray* for and *bless* others. Finally (and he had the most to say about this), priests should "let the Word of God dwell richly among them (Col. 3:16)," *reading Scripture* prayerfully and obediently under the inspiration of the Holy Spirit. It's one reason that the centerpiece of Spener's strategy for church renewal was to recover another idea of Luther's and found small group Bible studies: *ecclesiolae in ecclesia*, "little churches within the church."

Whatever Happened to the Common Priesthood?

This is a powerful vision for a church in which "each is given the manifestation of the Spirit for the common good," a body arranged so as to give "greater honor to the inferior member" (1 Cor 12:7, 24). But over a hundred years after Luther's death, German Pietists complained that Protestant churches had all but abandoned the common priesthood. Michelle Clifton-Soderstrom concludes that "the practice of faith was so limited to the clergy that not only did this bifurcate the common priesthood, it also became nearly impossible for the church to experience what Luther and Spener referred to as an enlivened faith." Francke was even more pointed about the elevation of powerful pastors above a passive laity: "What horrid Mischief this wicked distinction is the cause of."

The forgetting of the common priesthood helped produce what historians call the "crisis of piety" in seventeenth-century Europe. If we're facing a similar crisis here in twenty-first-century America—if too many Christians are acting like the functional atheists and fearful nonneighbors I described in chapter one—perhaps it's because we've again lost sight of the common priesthood.

Think about your own congregation. Do you see all believers sharing the priestly offices of sacrifice, prayer and blessing, and the Word? Or do you see most lay Christians ceding those responsibilities to pastors caught between the temptation of too much power and the weight of too many expectations? Or perhaps you're thinking of former members of your church who have drifted into the "spiritual but not religious" category, convinced that they can better follow Jesus' teachings apart from anything like the obligations and offices of institutional Christianity?

As I started to argue in chapter one, American Christians like me tend to conform ourselves to the values of our economy, rather than living out the countercultural values of the kingdom of God. This has implications for more than just the use of our time. It means that we're liable to have megachurch pastors who act like CEOs of Fortune 500 corporations and church planters who act like tech-sector entrepreneurs. It turns laypeople from full participants in the mission of the church into fickle consumers and idle spectators. The popular Christian writer Jen Hatmaker warns that such a framework "sets leaders and followers up for failure, creating a church-centric paradigm in which discipleship is staffled and program-driven. This slowly builds a consumer culture wherein spiritual responsibility is transferred from Christians to the pastors, a recipe for disaster."

So let's listen again to Spener, who insisted both that pastors were no higher in the priesthood than anyone else and that "the ministry cannot accomplish all that it ought [because] it is too weak without the help of the universal priesthood." Later Pietists continued to seek new ways of keeping all believers actively engaged in the common priesthood. I certainly wouldn't go as far as those Radical Pietists who did away with ordained clergy altogether. But I can't help but notice that the nineteenth-century revival that birthed the Evangelical Covenant Church had lay leaders such as C. O. Rosenius, who affirmed the office of pastors but taught followers like Mor i Vall that "*everyone* must preach with their *lives*."

From Presence to Practice: Priesthood Is Not Private

Here am I; send me!

ISAIAH 6:8

I once heard Mark preach on Isaiah 6:1-8, which unforgettably describes the call of one of the greatest Hebrew prophets. At least in this life, few of us in the common priesthood experience a divine encounter as dramatic as Isaiah's. But Mark observed that however we experience awe when we come into God's presence, it fundamentally changes what it means for us to join that prophet in responding to God's call:

> When we come before God, we find that everything else begins to fall into place. When we worship God as God, when we ultimately come before the awesome nature of God, then we begin to realize what's important in our lives and in our world. . . . [This awe] affects us so that we go out into the world, different than we were before, ready to live out, not just our purpose, not just seeking happiness for ourselves where we're the center of our universe, but going out to serve God and his purposes in this world, because we're not fearful.

"Going out" is the key phrase here. While Western Christians often understand holiness, prayer, and Bible study to be private and solitary, to serve in the common priesthood is also public and social. "Solitary Religion is not to be found" in the gospel, insisted John Wesley. "The Gospel of Christ knows of no Religion, but Social; no Holiness, but Social Holiness."

For as much as we can individually approach God "with a true heart in full assurance of faith" (Heb 10:22), we priests are called to make that faith active, to "provoke one another to love and good deeds" (Heb 10:24). "Let mutual love continue," concludes the author of Hebrews.

> Do not neglect to show hospitality to strangers, for by doing that some have entertained angels without knowing it. Remember those who are in prison, as though you were in prison with them; those who are being tortured, as though you yourselves were being tortured. Let marriage be held in honor by all, and let the marriage bed be kept undefiled; for God will judge fornicators and adulterers. (Heb 13:1-4)

If we sacrifice, it is not only for personal holiness but for the good of others (from strangers to spouses). If we pray, it is not only for ourselves but for others (from friends to enemies). And while we can dwell in the Word in the solitude of our own devotional time, we must remember that God inspired Scripture "so that everyone who belongs to God may be proficient, equipped for every good work" (2 Tim 3:16-17).

"It is," Spener concluded, Christians' "greatest joy to be occupied with their God and his Word (Ps. 119:102f)." But members of the common priesthood "still live in the world . . . and are also placed by God in certain positions for the general good." Or, as we tend to call it in our time, the common good.

Christ the Servant of Culture

Having loved his own who were in the world, [Jesus] loved them to the end.

JOHN 13:1

So how do Pietists do this? How do they engage in the common priesthood for the common good—not only that of fellow Christians, that is, but of our neighbors of other or no religion? For, as God said via another prophet, aren't we called to "seek the welfare of the city where I have sent you into exile, and pray to the LORD on its behalf, for in its welfare you will find your welfare" (Jer 29:7)?

Over the past two thousand years, Christians have adopted many strategies for relating to the world around them. In the influential 1951 book *Christ and Culture*, H. Richard Niebuhr described five basic types of relating to culture. At the extremes, he found that some Christians so

> While Western Christians often understand holiness, prayer, and Bible study to be private and solitary, to serve in the common priesthood is also public and social.

fully absorb prevailing values that they seem to believe in a "Christ of Culture," while others of their sisters and brothers reject many of the same values and distance themselves from the world ("Christ Against Culture"). In between these poles, Niebuhr observed three varieties of Christians who followed "Christ Above Culture," seeking in different ways to live in the world but not of it. While he presented biblical and historical precedents for each type, he seemed most inclined toward the idea of Christians being "transformers of culture," optimistically seeking to "carry out cultural work in obedience to the Lord."

Strikingly, Dale Brown concluded that the pietistic Christianity he had known in the Church of the Brethren didn't conform to any of Niebuhr's types. On the one hand, their Anabaptist roots led the Brethren to strive for nonconformity and to embrace suffering as a form of witness. But this "biblical realism" was tempered by their Pietist heritage, with its abiding hope centered on "the Spirit's power to both change persons and usher in better times for the world." (Similarly, here's how Brethren in Christ pastor Perry Engle describes the effects of Pietist revival on his Anabaptist forebears: "I like to think that these bold and serious-minded believers were 'sweetened' by their personal experience of a heartfelt and life-changing relationship with Christ.") So Brown proposed a "third way . . . neither to try to get on top in order to make things come out the way we think they should or refuse to become involved at all."

The Pietist option is to come back to the Jesus whom Brown called "Christ the Servant of culture." I don't think this precludes the other *Christ and Culture* types. Many of you reading this book may strive to transform culture, wherever you're called and with what gifts you're given. Others affirm Luther's paradox that Christians should neither compromise their citizenship in the kingdom of God nor ignore the necessary roles played by the kingdoms of this world. But Pietism can leaven such strategies, continually calling Christians back to the motivations and actions of the Servant who stooped to wash his disciples' feet— "For I have set you an example," Jesus told his flabbergasted followers, "that you also should do as I have done to you" (Jn 13:15).

> The Pietist option calls Christians back to the motivations and actions of the Servant who stooped to wash his disciples' feet.

What does this look like in practice? Consider some advice from Carl Lundquist, the Baptist pastor who served as president of Bethel College and Seminary from 1954 to 1982 and embodied the Pietist ethos as well as any other American evangelical leader. "Like our Savior," Lundquist once preached, "Christian students and teachers must be found among the poor, the disenfranchised, the needy, the infirm, the sinful, the greedy, the immoral, and the intoxicated." As much as he wanted Christians to strive for a personal holiness marked by "New Testament ideals of humility, modesty, and purity," he also affirmed theologian Donald Bloesch's call for "a holiness in the world, a piety that is to be lived out in the midst of the suffering and dereliction of men." In short, Lundquist hoped that Bethel graduates would be "seriously service motivated." While he no doubt had in mind the teachers, nurses, ministers, missionaries, and social workers for which Bethel is still well known, Lundquist also encouraged students to go into business, politics, and law—not to amass wealth or power, but because those too were "helping professions" in which they could "have maximum personal relationships."

Brown finds much the same attitude in the ministry of German Pietists such as Francke: "As a result of the emphasis on the love of God and neighbor, pietistic compassion highlighted the servant role." Whatever the job, taught Francke, the key is that the convert "carries out his professional calling joyfully and cheerfully to the glory of God and his neighbor's good without greed." And "if you cannot turn your profession itself to God's glory and neighbor's best, but rather it brings about your neighbor's harm, . . . you must also change your profession even though it may appear as hard to you as the command of Christ to the rich young man." Franke refers here to Jesus' command in Matthew 19:21: "If you wish to be perfect, go, sell your possessions, and give the money to the poor, and you will have treasure in heaven; then come, follow me." Whether in the corner office or the corridors of political power, the hospital or the home, Pietists glorify God by seeking their neighbors' good.

Both/And, Not Either-Or
If we model our contributions to the common good after the foot-washing example of Jesus, we should remember that the "suffering servant" will "not grow faint or be crushed until he has *established justice*

in the earth" (Is 42:4). We need to beware adopting what Brown calls "a Band-Aid approach which tries to patch up the devastating effects of injustice instead of getting at the root causes of our social maladies." It's a problem that our denomination named several years ago:

> We also confess that when we have cared for hurting people, we have been persistently reticent to address the causes that hurt people. We are more comfortable taking up the questions of compassion and mercy: "Who is broken? Who is in need?" We are less comfortable with those of justice: "Why does this brokenness exist? How do we address the causes?"

Such an imbalance isn't unique to Pietists. "Some churches preach truth by focusing on an individual approach to repentance and salvation," observes Covenant pastor Efrem Smith. "Or they only focus on sin issues such as fornication, murder, and adultery and leave racism, sexism, and oppression alone." (Of course, others "focus on issues like racism and sexism and give no attention to the biblical truth of the authority of Scripture or the necessity of the new birth.") The solution, Smith concludes, is to "connect truth, justice, and righteousness [Jer 4:2] in order to advance the Kingdom of God in these days and live out ancient biblical mandates."

> **Compassion and justice are causes and effects of each other in the kingdom of God.**

Fortunately, here the Pietist option doesn't require an either-or choice. First, if the common priesthood seeks the common good, justice need not be pitted against compassion. "Those who put on Band-Aids," Brown concludes in *Understanding Pietism*, "are likely to be moved to seek out the sources of infection. In fact, many who have sympathetically identified with the oppressed through a servant role have become the ones who are most existentially involved in the attacks on injustice." Compassion and justice are causes and effects of each other in the kingdom of God, where "steadfast love and faithfulness will meet; / righteousness and peace will kiss each other" (Ps 85:10).

Second, Pietists refuse to constrain the Christian life to the result of a choice between private devotion and public action. Instead, Pietists know that the two halves of their priestly calling reinforce each other. Those who come into the presence of God through prayer, study, and worship are then sent out, awestruck and inspired, to live in service to others.

For example, theologian Christian Collins Winn observes a "Pietist impulse to extend the care of the soul to include care for the body and society." He points in particular to the nineteenth-century German pastor Johann Christoph Blumhardt and his son, Christoph Friedrich Blumhardt, in whose healing ministry and political activism we can "find a convergence of spirituality and social action that is both spiritually rich and profoundly influential."

Writing in the era of the Vietnam War, Carl Lundquist encouraged the people of Bethel's denomination, the Baptist General Conference, "to identify with [the] valid emphases" of "the new American revolution," but also lamented that "an experience-centered genration [sic] of young people has not pursued deeply the inner resources to be found in Christian devotion." At the conclusion of a 1976 tour of "centers of Christian renewal" in Europe and America, Lundquist found in each place he visited that "social action—tender, loving care— became a normative expression of personal devotion to Christ." Lundquist would spend his post-Bethel retirement encouraging evangelicals to practice the spiritual disciplines, but he continued to believe that "pietism" and "activism" were interdependent—"the roots and fruit of the Christian faith."

CHAPTER 5

Christianity as Life

Although Spener was formally orthodox in his theology, his greatest interest was not in orthodoxy of doctrine. Instead, the emphasis of his ministry moved toward practice. . . . [The Pietists] did not desire to disparage doctrine; they insisted that doctrine encompass life.

Dale W. Brown, *Understanding Pietism*

I (Mark) still remember reading the book in my first term of seminary. I had studied some church history during my undergraduate years and had even joined an Evangelical Covenant church, yet somehow the term *Pietism* had never quite registered in my mind. As I read Donald Frisk's *The New Life in Christ*, I not only became aware of the presence of the Pietists in history and their influence on the theology and practice of my new church family, but I also found my heart swelling with excitement as I saw in his words a simple articulation of the Christ-centered faith, theology, and mission I held dear. As I read Frisk's words, I came to understand that I was a Pietist.

> Christianity is essentially a personal relationship to God, through faith in Jesus Christ, which makes a difference in one's life. Pietism and subsequent movements influenced by it demonstrate a strong and persistent drive to press through the unessential to the indispensable center of Christianity—the new life in Christ. . . .

Accordingly, our forefathers rarely asked, when they met their friends and neighbors, "What do you believe?" But sooner or later they were sure to ask, "Are you alive spiritually?" "Have you found life in Christ?" "Have you met him and found your life changed through faith in him?"

Christianity is life. Not primarily a system of beliefs or doctrines, but a way of life—indeed, *the Way*, to use terminology by which the earliest Christians described their venture together in Christ (e.g., Acts 9:2; 18:25-26; 19:9). Intellectual assent to various propositions—though they be true, though you believe them—is not enough. "It is by no means enough to have knowledge of the Christian faith, for Christianity consists rather of practice," wrote Philipp Spener. This is not to suggest that intellectual belief and understanding are not important. It is to say that what we are offered in Christ and called to do for Christ is all that and much more.

A Living Faith: Head, Heart, and Hands

Spener and the other early Pietists argued for a greater integration of intellectual belief, heartfelt commitment, and the practical living out of one's faith in love. Pietists are inclined toward a both/and perspective, as Chris noted in the previous chapter. In this case, "and" ties together not just two but three foundational elements of what the Pietists called a *living faith*. To put it simply, such a faith engages and enlivens one's head *and* heart *and* hands.

Engaging the head. A living faith is not a blind one. Engaging our heads means that our faith has to make sense to us on an intellectual level. As a pastor and preacher, I regularly take time to study yet again whether the evidence available is adequate to support my faith. I have to know with integrity in my mind that I believe what I'm preaching. And while all may not wrestle as regularly as I do, we all need to have our heads fully on board if we are to surrender ourselves fully to the extraordinary claims and call of the gospel.

Engaging our minds also means going beyond wrestling with *whether* we believe to clarifying *what* we believe. Despite what many seem to assume in our culture, not every idea is as good as the next. Even when it takes the name "Christian," not every notion about God, path to spiritual vitality, or religious tradition is as healthy as the next.

What and how we think matters. Simply looking at the evils perpetrated in the name of various belief systems—religious or otherwise, by freelancing terrorists or nation-states—is enough to make this point clear. It is not enough to simply feel the impulse of faith in your heart. How those impulses are encouraged, discouraged, and given guidance by our heads makes a world of difference.

The early Pietists encouraged rigorous academic study and thoughtful discernment. Such discernment is necessary, especially in polarized times. Our personal experience, biases, and emotions can so easily cloud our judgment and lead us astray. We need to continually use our heads to increase our self-awareness, decrease our reactivity, listen to and consider differing perspectives, and exercise self-control. It is true, Frisk admits, that Pietists have sometimes been tempted to focus on "'religious experience' simply for its own sake." However, he makes it clear that

> wiser heads did not deny the central place of the objective aspect of the Christian message. . . . They knew that their experience of salvation was possible only on the basis of the objective action of God on behalf of mankind through the life, death, and resurrection of Jesus Christ. . . . They had no basic quarrel with the theological statements of the day or with the need of discipline and order within the church. Their concern was that men believe not only with the head but with the heart as well.

Engaging the heart. This "with the heart as well" is a distinctive emphasis of the Pietists. A living faith must certainly engage the head, but also the heart. At the time the Pietist movement came into being, Lutheran orthodoxy treated faith as "a noun, something (a body of propositions) with which one agreed," writes Gary Sattler. "For [August Hermann] Francke faith was a verb, a way of being which was the necessary outworking of intellectual and emotional assent to the claim that Jesus is Savior."

The necessary outworking of one's faith only truly flows when the heart is fully engaged. What is needed is not just the assent of one's mind but also the conversion of one's heart. Spener quoted from Martin Luther's preface to his commentary on Romans to make this point: "When they hear the gospel, they go ahead and by their own powers fashion an idea in their hearts which says, 'I believe.' This they hold for true faith. But it is a human imagination and idea that never reaches the depths of the heart, and so nothing comes of it and no betterment follows it." For Spener, we need a "heart ready to do the divine will," writes Covenant theologian John Weborg.

One woman in our congregation described the shift toward a deeper motivation in this way: "A lot of churches have made me a better person, a nicer person, a better rule follower. This church has helped me just fall in love with the person of Jesus."

The loving engagement of the heart is life giving and motivational beyond rational explanation, as many great leaders have known. It is true that there are dangers in going too far in the "touchy-feely" or mystical direction. But it is well worth acknowledging that there are dangers in the other direction as well. When we try to limit what we will allow God to do in us to what we can fully understand, articulate, or control, we are not open to all the ways God might want to transform and use us.

For some, this practice of allowing, even inviting, God to touch and transform our emotions comes more easily than for others. Yet the need is present for all. And for all of us it is important to remember that we are better together than apart. Together, by God's grace, we can both help each other open our hearts and help each other guard against unhealthy extremes. It is a bit risky and maybe uncomfortable, but offering both the head and the heart to God is necessary for an integrated, living faith.

Engaging the hands. Engaging the heart along with the head was a key emphasis for the early Pietists. It is clear, though, that their ultimate aim was a life transformed. They fully believed that real and lasting fruit is not only possible but to be expected. A faith that makes sense in one's head and even brings warm sentiment to the heart is still not a living faith unless it makes a difference in how one lives.

Here again, Spener quotes Luther: "Faith, however, is a divine work in us. It changes us and makes us to be born anew of God (John 1:13). It kills the old Adam and makes altogether different men of us in heart and spirit and mind and powers and it brings with it the Holy Spirit. O, it is a living, busy, active, mighty thing, this faith, and so it is impossible for it not to do good works incessantly." Practically speaking, finding "it impossible for it not to do good works incessantly" may seem a bit of a stretch for those of us still weighed down by our sinful natures. But the point is clear. A living faith—one that is continuing to grow according to God's formative power—bears fruit. It shows up in how life is lived, in what the hands do.

> A faith that makes sense in one's head and brings warm sentiment to the heart is not a living faith unless it makes a difference in how one lives.

As noted at the beginning of this chapter, Spener attested that "it is by no means enough to have knowledge of the Christian faith, for Christianity consists rather of practice." Significantly, he follows this statement by clearly pointing out what that practice looks like: "Our dear Savior repeatedly enjoined love as the real mark of his disciples (John 13:34-35, 15:12; 1 John 3:10, 18, 4:7-8, 11-13, 21). . . . Indeed, love is the whole command of the man who has faith and who through his faith is saved, and his fulfillment of the laws of God consists of love."

To understand fully Spener's call to practice love, remember that he was born during the Thirty Years' War and wrote *Pia Desideria* in its aftermath. It was a highly polarized time. The peace was tenuous. Territorial, societal, and ecclesial boundaries were becoming increasingly rigid throughout central Europe. Having grown up in the borderlands between Germany and France, Spener understood deeply what it meant to straddle highly charged dividing lines. He had seen neighbors turn violently upon neighbors. He knew what it was like for people to be inclined toward vengeance rather than neighborly love.

This was the context in which Spener appealed to the church to "awaken a fervent love among our Christians, first toward one another and then toward all men . . . and put this love into practice." What is all the more remarkable given the polarized time in which he lived was that he called people to practice this love *especially* by "seek[ing] opportunities to do good to their enemies in order that such self-control may hurt the old Adam, who is otherwise inclined to vengeance." In our own polarized times, this call to make such love our practice is crucial.

How Goes Your Walk?

Teach me, where'er Thy steps I see,
Dauntless, untired, to follow Thee:
O let Thy hand support me still,
And lead me to Thy holy hill.

NIKOLAUS VON ZINZENDORF

When Jesus started his ministry, he started calling people to walk with him. Writing of C. O. Rosenius and P. P. Waldenstrom, two leaders in the Pietist revival of nineteenth-century Sweden, Mark Safstrom notes that both "were concerned first and foremost in cultivating an abiding and living faith among their readers and parishioners, regardless of denominational affiliation. Two questions that were ubiquitous in the communities that these preachers served were 'How goes your walk with the Lord?' and 'Are you living yet/still in Jesus?'"

Their questions came to mind a few years ago while I was on a retreat in the Sonoran Desert near Tucson, Arizona. On my first afternoon, after walking silently through the desert for about twenty minutes, I found an old African American spiritual arising in my spirit:

I want Jesus to walk with me.
All along my pilgrim journey;
Lord, I want Jesus to walk with me.

It seemed the perfect prayer for the day, the retreat, and my life.

The next afternoon I ventured out in silence again. After about twenty minutes, without forethought or planning on my part, a slightly different version of the song arose within me. I found myself singing, "I want Mark to walk with me. I want Mark to walk with me . . ."

I recognize that the slaves who first sang the song had little choice as to the direction they might walk. The words were a plaintive cry for Jesus to walk with them amid their suffering and pain. As such, it continues to have a deep resonance for many in times of distress.

For me, though, walking that afternoon as a well-off white American enjoying the second day of a sabbatical, I was aware that the options as to which way I might go were plentiful—not only there as I explored the desert but in all of life. My need was not just for Jesus to walk with me but, far more, for me to learn to walk with him and follow his way.

As the words "I want Mark to walk with me" came out of my mouth, they seemed to be arising from the heart of God. I was struck that long before I had dreamed of inviting Jesus to walk with me, he'd been singing this song of love and invitation to me. With each of our own names inserted, this is the song the Trinity—the Father, Son, and Holy Spirit— has been singing since before the creation of the world.

Jesus didn't come to punch our eternal train ticket to heaven so that we can just live with him there. Nor did he come simply to tag along wherever we choose to go. No, the critical invitation is the one Jesus extends to all his disciples: "Follow me!" (e.g., Mt 4:19). The walk of faith is not one in which Jesus simply walks our way, carelessly blessing our self-centered activities and inclinations. The walk with the Lord to which we are invited is one in which he leads and we learn with him the pathway of peace.

The Journey Inward

Prayer is to look to the omnipresent God and to allow oneself to be seen by him. What is now easier and more simple than to turn our eyes upward and to see the light which surrounds us on all sides? God is far more present to us than the light. In him we live, we move, and we are. He penetrates us, he fills us, he is nearer to us than we are to ourselves. To believe this in simplicity and to think of this simply as well as one can, that is prayer. How can it be difficult to allow oneself to be looked after by so kind a physician, who knows better what is troubling us than we ourselves know? We have no need to bring this or that, to present ourselves in this way or in that way, or to look too much, or to experience much, if we wish to pray, but we need only simply and briefly to say how we are and how we wish to be; indeed, it is not even necessary that we say this, but we need only allow the ever-present good God to see.

GERHARD TERSTEEGEN

Walking with Jesus first takes us on a journey inward, allowing him full access to the inner person. Spener advised his readers to "accustom the people first to work on what is inward (awaken love of God and neighbor through suitable means) and only then to act accordingly."

The first step of this walk is rest. It's instructive that while the sabbath day of rest in the creation story was the seventh day for God, it was the first full day for Adam and Eve (Gen 2:2-3). They began their journey in life with rest. In like manner, the beginning of each day for the Jewish people comes at sundown, the time human beings have generally understood as the time for rest. The pattern is clear: God's people begin by resting in God's faithful care.

In this sense, the first and most central purpose of prayer is simply to rest and be receptive in the presence of God. We are like the solar-powered crafts that have been sent into the far reaches of space. They are carefully and wonderfully made at great expense. They are created to accomplish great things and fulfill breathtaking missions. Yet their first and continual task is to open their solar panels wide and position themselves toward the sun, the source of their power. Apart from that they can do nothing—something Jesus tells us is precisely what happens to us if we are not abiding in him (Jn 15:5).

For me centering prayer has become a foundational practice. I take time each day to simply be still before God, to present myself before God and practice being present to the One who is always present in love to me. My intention is to make like a sunflower that continually turns its face toward the sun, positioning myself in a receptive manner toward God as I begin my devotional time and as I continue through the day.

Whatever the devotional practices we incorporate into the daily, weekly, and ongoing rhythm of our lives, it is crucial that we recognize them as opportunities to rest in and receive God's grace. We are not only saved by God's grace; we are also enabled by it to live out our salvation, our new life in Christ. As the apostle Paul makes clear, it is God who is at work in us, enabling us both to will and to work for God's good pleasure (Phil 2:12-13).

Both Scripture and church history witness to the extraordinary fruitfulness of a life prayerfully centered in God. Yet many of us find it difficult. Most of us struggle at least occasionally, if not more often, to offer our limited and therefore precious time to God through regular devotional practices. However, to the degree we believe in the God of the Scriptures and the teachings of Jesus, our belief must drive us to turn our attention toward God, toward Jesus, toward the Source of the life we've been given. Otherwise, in practical terms we are operating like Adam and Eve, who fell prey to the temptation to try to "be like God" (Gen 3:5). Then, rather than looking to and relying on God, our actions show that we think we can live this God-given life in our own wisdom and power.

It is not just Pietists who understand how crucial it is that Christians prioritize and practice this inward journey, not instead of the outward one but as an inseparable characteristic of a whole and healthy, fruitful life. Catholic mystic Richard Rohr writes,

> Over the years I met many social activists who were doing excellent social analysis and advocating for crucial justice issues, but they were not working from an energy of love except in their own minds. They were still living out of their false self with the need to win, the need to look good, the attachment to a superior, politically correct self-image. . . . That's one reason that most revolutions fail. Too many reformers self-destruct from within. For that very reason, I believe, Jesus and great spiritual teachers first emphasize transformation of consciousness and soul.

To be clear, the invitation to the journey inward is not a call to work harder at prayer, meditation, memorization and study of Scripture, journaling, and the like. These practices and others are all means by which we can open our lives to the transforming grace of God. But our receptivity is limited when we approach these activities as work to do rather than ways by which we may receive grace. In the first case, our devotional exercises simply make us busier and prouder. In the latter, our spiritual practices become means by which we welcome the very presence and grace of God.

The Journey Outward

Whatever form conversion takes it will be characterized by entrance into *freedom*—**the freedom which comes through the presence of Christ in one's life**—**and by** *involvement* **in Christ's mission to the world. To be converted to Christ is always in a sense to be converted (turned) to the world. It is to see the world through the eyes of Christ, to share his compassion, to perceive his will for the world, and to strive to follow it.**

DON FRISK

Conversion is not frequently thought of as a turning outward to the world. More often we think of it as a turning toward God, and rightly so. Yet turning *to* God also means turning *with* God to see and serve the world. As we have celebrated and soaked in the love of Jesus for us on our journey inward, so we begin to notice and be caught up in his abounding love for others.

Following Jesus, we follow his gaze as he looks out on the world with love. Walking with Jesus, we walk with him in extending his love to our neighbors. Loving Jesus, we love him among those with whom he promised he would be—the hungry, thirsty, strangers, naked, sick, and imprisoned. When we come back to Jesus, we experience not only the joy of receiving his love but the joy of coming alongside him in loving others.

Expressing our love for Jesus by turning our attention toward our neighbors is imperative, as Spener understood: "All the commandments are summed up in love (Rom. 13:9). Accordingly the people are not only to be told this incessantly, and they are not only to have the excellence of neighborly love and, on the other hand, the great danger and

harm in the opposing self-love pictured impressively before their eyes
. . . , but they also must practice such love."

In contrast, Western Christians today are often stirred up not to
"love and good deeds" (Heb 10:24) but to fear, emotional reactivity,
and hate. It is a dangerous and clearly un-Christ-like path. Yet it is
one we are continually tempted to take. The Thirty Years' War served as
the early Pietists' prime example of this road not to be taken. They'd
seen far too many of those calling themselves by the name of Christ
swept up in attitudes and actions nowhere near those exemplified and
taught by him. They'd witnessed far too many neighbors caught up in
serving out violence to neighbor rather than love. For us, the past
century has been replete with such examples, and our current landscape of polarizing politics seems only
to be encouraging us in that destructive direction.

> We love Jesus among those with whom he promised he would be—the hungry, thirsty, strangers, naked, sick, and imprisoned.

My own family's experience of the very real danger of this downward
path toward hatred and violence is significant. As I mentioned in chapter
two, most of my mother's family was lost a century ago, as neighbor
turned on neighbor in the extermination of over a million Armenians.
A Christian minority, Armenians had for centuries lived in relative peace
and close interaction with their Turkish and Kurdish neighbors. This
was at least in part because of the Qur'an's teaching that Muslims should
look after "the people of the book."

In the years leading up to World War I, however, the emotional state
of those in the majority became inflamed, fanned by those in power, and
directed in an inhuman direction. As in the case of so many other un-
thinkable atrocities, the majority was not under any realistic threat from
the minority. Yet the latter became the locus of all the former's anxieties
about the changes and challenges they faced. Their Armenian neighbors

became the feared "other," the scapegoats for every problem. My sister, a cultural anthropologist who has studied Armenian communities, concludes, "Neighbors who had known each other became strangers. More importantly, for Turks and Kurds, Armenians were no longer humans but pests. For Armenians, these former neighbors became inhuman. In many ways, the word *enemy* is not sufficient to convey the fury of mass murder of civilians."

This scenario may seem a distant reality for many, but the rhetoric of today's politically charged atmosphere places the same issues at our front door. Fear, greed, ethnic and racial divisions, nationalism—all this and more tempts us to move away from rather than toward each other. The impulse to distrust, dismiss, and divide is as present in the church as elsewhere. Jesus calls us to make a countercultural move: to walk with him in love toward one another in the church and toward our neighbors beyond. "If there appears to be doubt whether or not one is obligated to do this or that out of love for one's neighbor," Spener concluded, "it is always better to incline toward doing it."

> Our world needs a new narrative to unite us in spirit and mission, to provide us a hopeful pathway to pursue together.

Our world needs a new narrative to unite us in spirit and mission, to provide us a hopeful pathway to pursue together. Jesus Christ offers just the hope-filled story we need. He invites us to walk with him into a future that his resurrection has already assured. He proclaims today, as he did long ago, "The time is fulfilled, and the kingdom of God has come near; repent, and believe in the good news. . . . Follow me" (Mk 1:15, 17).

The resurrection of Jesus Christ has given us a glimpse of a glorious future beyond any apparent horizon of failure, humiliation, and even death. We know that, like the Pietists before us, we will not get it right every time. We are aware that even our best efforts will always fall short. Yet, as the apostle Paul urges, we venture forward boasting "in our hope of sharing the glory of God" (Rom 5:2).

The Way Forward

Therefore, my beloved, be steadfast, immovable, always excelling in the work of the Lord, because you know that in the Lord your labor is not in vain.

1 CORINTHIANS 15:58

We are vulnerable and dependent on God. Left to our own knowledge, power, and purity, we can never guarantee success and invincibility for ourselves, those we love, or the institutions we care about. Moreover, following Jesus' path of love will entail more vulnerability, not less. In the face of our fears, anxieties, and vulnerability, we must choose to move forward, confident in our hope, bearing the fruit of love. As we do, we can be assured about the prepositions by which we've come to experience God. We venture into the future confident that God is *with* us, *for* us, *in* us, *among* us, and working *through* us. It is in this confidence that we can boldly risk following Jesus' way of love.

We must continually make it our aim to live out our new life in Christ. Even those deeply shaped by a Pietist heritage are prone to slip into the old, seemingly wise, seductive attitudes of cynicism, narcissism, and despair. There is nothing lovely or God-honoring about these attitudes. There is nothing in them "worthy of praise" (Phil 4:8). None of them reflects the sense of gratitude, humility, and joy—let alone faith, hope, and love—characteristic of Pietism. With Paul, Pietists such as Spener, Waldenström, and Frisk would caution us to strip "off the old self with its practices" and clothe "yourselves with the new self" (Col 3:9-10).

But they'd also remind us that we can't live this life by ourselves. The Scriptures are clear that all who through faith have been united with Christ have been united with one another. We need each other—and not just in confronting the biggest, most divisive issues of our day. We also need one another in the day-to-day practice of the Christian life. One of the keys to the Pietists' renewal movement was their commitment to gathering together in small groups to pray, to read the Scriptures and reflect on them, and to encourage one another in living out their faith.

We are individual members of one body, and, as in every body, there is an ongoing tension between the members' needs to individuate and to remain connected. Health is not achieved by choosing one or the other but by continuing to acknowledge and graciously wrestle with the tension. "Bear with one another," Paul admonishes us, "forgive each other. . . . Above all, clothe yourselves in love, which binds everything together in perfect harmony. And let the peace of Christ rule in your hearts, to which you were indeed called in the one body" (Col 3:13-15). These practices, along with the fruit of the Spirit (Gal 5:22-23), are the true signs of new life in Christ.

CHAPTER 6

The Irenic Spirit

Unity, Mission, and Witness

When my wife and I (Chris) got married, we asked friends to read two Scriptures. The first was Psalm 100. Besides being a great song of worship and thanksgiving, it contains a profound statement of who we are, and whose: "Know that the LORD is God. / It is he that made us, and we are his; / we are his people, and the sheep of his pasture" (Ps 100:3). Especially at a wedding, the accents land on the plurals: he made *us*; *we* are his *people*. And that should remind us that God made humanity in a particular way: "Then God said, 'Let us make humankind in *our* image, according to *our* likeness. . . . In the image of God he created *them*; male and female he created *them*" (Gen 1:26-27). This truth has helped inspire a widespread belief in the equality, dignity, and freedom of every single person alive. But we should not think only of individuals when we consider the *imago Dei*. God made people to relate to God and to each other. Moreover, Christians believe that God is not solitary but triune: three persons united as one.

So we bear this image most fully when we are together with others: distinct, yet unified. Or as our second wedding text put it: "If then there is any encouragement in Christ, any consolation from love, any sharing in the Spirit, any compassion and sympathy, make my joy complete: be of the same mind, having the same love, being in full accord and of one mind" (Phil 2:1-2). It's a good word for a couple to hear as they begin their life together. But Paul meant it for a larger community of believers. Would that more churches and Christian organizations took it as seriously as they take their stances on marriage!

Instead, "making every effort to maintain the unity of the Spirit in the bond of peace" (Eph 4:3) seems like the easiest platitude to mouth and the easiest conviction to set aside. But the Pietist option is to insist that unity—while impossible to achieve perfectly—is essential to Christian community, mission, and witness.

We're Better Together Than Apart

Of its four defining instincts, the impulse to stay together is the one that first drew me to Pietism. Between the ages of sixteen and twenty-four I experienced three church schisms. In each case, each side thought it had biblically based, Christ-centered reasons to split; not one of those congregations has yet to recover from the experience. And too often it seemed that many other churches that avoided such splits did so by substituting political, racial, or socioeconomic uniformity for Christian unity.

So when I came to Bethel University, my ears perked up as I heard colleagues talk about the university's "irenic spirit." Here were evangelical Baptists who wanted to be known not for schism, heresy hunting, or culture warring but as a peaceable, open-minded people who built a diverse learning community around shared devotion to Jesus Christ.

At the same time, with my return to the denomination of my childhood I gained new appreciation that the Covenant Church holds only five broad doctrinal affirmations, plus a sixth that grants "freedom in Christ":

> With a modesty born of confidence in God, Covenanters have offered to one another theological and personal freedom where the biblical and historical record seems to allow for a variety of interpretations of the will and purposes of God. . . . This commitment to freedom has kept the Covenant Church together when it would have been easier to break fellowship and further divide Christ's body.

It's not like Pietist communities don't experience conflict. (Even as we write, Bethel and the Covenant Church are debating everything from sexuality and marriage to racial justice and immigration.) But the more I began to dig into the histories of these institutions, the more I saw the enduring influence of a religious ethos that takes seriously the New Testament's exhortations to Christian unity.

Born during the bloodiest European war before the twentieth century, Philipp Spener advised German-speaking Christians caught in the middle of interdenominational bickering to avoid needless controversy. For even if arguing about doctrine could bring about a "conviction of truth," warned Spener in *Pia Desideria*, it "is far from being faith. Faith requires more." Debates of this sort are as likely to result in dead orthodoxy as living faith, so it became clear to Spener that "disputing is not enough either to maintain the truth among ourselves or to impart it to the erring."

Instead, Spener, a Lutheran pastor, welcomed Christians of other confessions into his small group studies. Spener even wondered whether it might not be possible to bridge divides more permanently:

> If there is any prospect of a union of most of the confessions among Christians, the primary way of achieving it, and the one that God would bless most, would perhaps be this, that we do not stake everything on argumentation, for the present disposition of men's minds, which are filled by as much fleshly as spiritual zeal, makes disputation fruitless.

Later Pietists shared the same hope. In the eighteenth century, Spener's godson Nikolaus von Zinzendorf attempted (unsuccessfully) to bring about such an ecumenical union. In the nineteenth century, the Swedish revivalist C. O. Rosenius contended that it was "the duty and wisdom of every Christian, as far as it is possible, to seek to unify and keep together this band of siblings, which is so often tempted to break apart."

Introducing a new evangelical journal called *Pietisten* in 1842, Rosenius (a Lutheran) and British missionary George Scott (a Methodist) emphasized that "doctrines of lesser importance" ought not to divide those seeking revival. "We love to understand pietism," they wrote, "as something, which belongs to the whole world, and not just part of it, as something common and accessible for all confessions, which hold themselves to Christ the head." This does not mean that Pietists are indifferent to doctrine. (In addition to its six distinctive affirmations, the Covenant Church affirms the historic creeds and the *solas* of the Reformation;

Bethel is sponsored by a noncreedal Baptist denomination, Converge Worldwide, but expects faculty and staff to support its twelve-point affirmation of faith.) But the vast majority of theological differences shouldn't stop Christians from worshiping and working together.

If Pietists are right that Christianity is primarily about not what we think about God but how we relate to God and what we do in his name, then perhaps common experience and common activity are healthier bases for unity than common belief. For example, first in Sweden (1878) and then in America (1885) some Rosenian Pietists formed "mission covenants." Whatever their theological differences, congregations worked together in order to engage in tasks that were too difficult to accomplish in isolation: bringing the gospel to those who had never heard it, caring for the sick and the elderly, and educating future pastors.

So there's practical value in working together on the particular aspects of our mission. But the unity of the church is much more than an alliance of convenience. (After all, as a businessman friend once told me, *partner* is another word for *competitor*.) Early Covenanters called themselves "Mission Friends," testifying to the fact that Christians' unity— *who* they are—is inseparable from Christians' mission—*what* they are called to do in this world.

Unity as Mission

At the end of his life, Jesus declared his disciples his friends, meaning they shared with him a common passion for his mission in the world (John 15:13-15). Covenanters, as Mission Friends, have broadly understood mission to be the befriending of others, and all that God has created, in the name of the One who first befriended us.

COVENANT AFFIRMATIONS

We bear the image of God most fully when we are together, to the extent that we have "the same love" and are "in full accord and of one mind." Conversely, we feel distortion of this image most keenly when love, accord, and unity are lost. And we sense this loss often. For what is the fall but this: created for relationship, we were made strangers to our Creator and to each other? Because of sin, we are prone to see God and everyone made in his image with fear and suspicion rather than awe and wonder.

But because Jesus Christ "died for all, so that those who live might live no longer for themselves," we, members of his body, "regard no one from a human point of view" (2 Cor 5:15-16). With the eyes of Christ, we see everyone made in God's image as a stranger to be welcomed (Mt 25:35). After all, Jesus asked, "If you greet only your brothers and sisters, what more are you doing than others?" (Mt 5:47). But speaking in his name, now we tell even our enemies, "It is well that you have come into our lives."

> A missional church should take the shape of an ever-widening circle of ever-deepening intimacy, with Jesus Christ at its center.

It is well: what was sick is being healed; what was broken is being made whole.

So what is our mission if not "the befriending of others . . . in the name of the One who first befriended us"? How can we engage in such reconciliation if members of our own body readily accept estrangement from each other? If the Great Commandment ("love the Lord your God . . . love your neighbor as yourself," Mk 12:30-31) animates the Great Commission ("Go therefore and make disciples of all nations," Mt 28:19), then a missional church should take the shape of an ever-widening circle of ever-deepening intimacy, with Jesus Christ at its center.

Unity as Witness

Jesus told his first followers, "You will be my witnesses in Jerusalem, in all Judea and Samaria, and to the ends of the earth" (Acts 1:8). As heirs of that charge, we can bear no better witness than to "become completely one, so that the world may know that you have sent me and have loved them even as you have loved me" (Jn 17:23). To strive for unity is to show a watching world an image of a three-in-one God whose members are different yet "completely one."

As it's translated in the Greek Septuagint, Genesis 1 describes humans as being made in the *eikon* (image) of God. And it's the story of a particular Greek icon that may be the most powerful metaphor I know for the relationship between Christian unity and Christian witness.

Journalist Andy Crouch tells of visiting an Eastern Orthodox monastery on the island of Patmos. While the monastery was named for John, who received his apocalyptic visions there, the greatest icon in its collection depicts two other apostles: Peter and Paul, embracing in something like what the latter called a "holy kiss" (Rom 16:16). A local scholar informed Crouch that the icon symbolizes *synaspismos*: an "ancient battle practice of advancing with shields overlapping one another, just as the saints overlap in this moment of greeting. It is a word for shared strength, comradeship and partnership—the sharing of power that enabled both Peter and Paul to fulfill their vocations as ambassadors of the gospel across the Roman Empire."

But Crouch notes that the apostles exchange a "somber, even a bit suspicious" expression. After all, the icon is meant to depict "very recent enemies meeting shortly after Paul's conversion from persecutor of the church to energetic defender of the Way of Jesus." This is a fresh befriending, both exciting and uncomfortable. And we know that even as their relationship deepened, their *synaspismos* was never entirely free of conflict (see Gal 2:11-14). So for Crouch, the icon is "a picture of fellowship, partnership and community, and also of difference, distance and difficulty. Ultimately they are all part of the same thing."

This is the complicated *eikon* that a united church has to show to a world, for our neighbors' good and to God's glory. "Icons," concludes Crouch, "are not meant primarily to be looked *at*; they are meant to be looked *through* . . . to invite us into a relationship with the One who drew Peter and Paul together, held them in fellowship in spite of themselves, and through them began to build one holy, catholic and apostolic church."

Advice for Unity

In the Christian congregation . . . a melting together is supposed to happen, in which all the differences of class and nation are supposed to disappear. Even if it goes slowly, it happens nonetheless—and it is surely happening. . . . For wherever on earth believers meet together, they feel themselves drawn together as brothers and sisters. This is God's love in Christ Jesus, which makes them soft and melts away that which previously held them at a distance from one another.

PAUL PETER WALDENSTRÖM

"Above all," urged the apostle Peter, "love each other deeply, because love covers over a multitude of sins" (1 Pet 4:8 NIV). Love each other, above all! So what does this mean in practice? If you resonate with the Pietist commitment to Christian unity, how can you help to work out this mutual love in your communities of faith?

And I do mean *work*. Remember, Paul said we'd have to make every effort to maintain this unity. The softening and melting that Covenant founder P. P. Waldenström celebrated "is surely happening"—but not easily, not quickly. So let's close with three pieces of advice.

Keep in mind that unity and conflict are not mutually exclusive. At its worst, the Pietist instinct to stay together just lets me feel self-righteous about one of my most problematic character traits: conflict avoidance. Intellectually I know that disagreement is normal, but the mere thought of confrontation is enough to start my Midwestern, Swedish American stomach churning.

But if Spener is right that we should avoid needless controversy, then that implies that some controversy is actually needful. So we ought to take seriously Baptist ethicist David Gushee's warning that, for the sake of maintaining unity, Christians can try "so hard to avoid controversy that the congregation, denomination, parachurch organization, or college is reduced to paralyzed silence, vague platitudes, and a constant effort not to talk about critical issues (and suffering people) that really demand reflection and response." If unity is held together by silence, it's no unity at all.

Instead, it's a counterfeit called uniformity. And that's detrimental to the healthy functioning of any Christian community or organization.

Anyone who has been part of a ministry staff, a church leadership team, or a small group study knows that like-mindedness can stifle generative conversations, silence cautionary dissent, and extinguish creative proposals before they have a chance to develop. Moreover, Christian communities that mistake ethnic, economic, or ideological sameness for unity can inadvertently hinder their mission. Social psychologist Christena Cleveland warns that such churches "are at great risk of engaging in groupthink as they make decisions on how to best impact society. The more we interact with those who are different, the more we can respond to the needs of those who are different."

> If unity is held together by silence, it's no unity at all.

Pietists have understood this, even as they heeded Spener's warnings against "angry disputation." Heading Sweden's rather ecumenical revival in the nineteenth century, C. O. Rosenius kept a commitment to unity that flowed out of his openness to disagreement: "Since we have a tendency to either lean to one side or the other, then it is quite healthy for us to keep company with brothers who have the opposite opinion from us." Or as C. J. Nyvall, one of the first Rosenian Pietists to travel to America, put it, "Peace within the group does not mean that all think alike and interpret all things alike, each wishing to see, as it were, his own self in another, but it does mean that each one recognizes his brother *in Christ*, whatever else the condition may be."

Paul taught the church in Corinth, "You are the body of Christ and individually members of it" (1 Cor 12:27)—all having different abilities, passions, roles, and perspectives. Note that when Paul urges a body toward unity, he emphasizes that it is unity in the Spirit. The Spirit, writes Pope Francis, "brings forth a rich variety of gifts, while at the same time creating a unity which is never uniformity but a multifaceted and inviting harmony." It is a unity in which we "see others in their deepest dignity"—a dignity rooted in their bearing the image of God—and thereby seek "reconciled diversity."

Kathy Khang argues that the differences between us do matter "because there is space to delight in the variety, creativity and abundance that is from God. Look around. God doesn't paint all the leaves one shade yellow." But in the end, she concludes, "Our differences don't define us; our Creator does." Unity doesn't preclude conflict, and fear of conflict shouldn't stop us from embracing diversity.

Recognize that unity is not the enemy of conviction. Trusting that we're better together than apart is an instinct—a fallible but deep-seated emotional impulse. But if it can steer us wrong, it can also counteract other fallible religious instincts—for example, the one that tempts some Christians to think that the chief proof of biblical faith is always to hold defiantly to one's convictions.

> When others have been too prone to say, "Here I stand," and accept schism, Pietists have wanted to ask, "Can we do other?"

Pietism shares with other Protestant traditions a commitment to the authority of Scripture alone, without giving a church hierarchy or a traditional interpretation the power to settle debates. Like Martin Luther before them, Protestants bind their individual consciences to God's Word alone, even to the point of breaking fellowship with others who are trying to do the same thing. But when other post-Reformation cousins have been too prone to say, "Here I stand," and accept schism, Pietists have wanted to ask, "Can we do other?"

"Here I stand" might feel more emotionally satisfying than the subtle, slow-arriving, and inevitably compromised joys of consensus—but that feeling isn't always trustworthy. First, it tends to produce a kind of tunnel vision, blinding us to other possibilities. Worse yet, it replaces self-awareness with self-righteousness as we forget that conviction is less a belief we decide to hold firmly than something that happens to us— God's work of convincing us of our sin, reminding us that we still "see in a mirror, dimly" and "know only in part" (1 Cor 13:12).

That doesn't mean that the Pietist's conscience isn't captive to the Word of God. But Pietists know that such a conviction requires humility, a readiness to bend the knee to Scripture as we read it together.

In the Covenant we hold that "the only perfect rule for faith, doctrine, and conduct" is the Bible itself—not any one person's interpretation of the Bible.

Conviction of this sort requires more patience. But if any issue is meaningful enough to inspire conviction, shouldn't it sustain more conversation, not less?

Unity is a task of Christian formation. None of this is easy to do, even in the best of circumstances. And we're not living in the best of circumstances. Given all the political, social, and cultural forces pulling us apart, we need to accept two hard facts. First, it will take time to achieve a greater degree of Christian unity; this is a long-term project. And second, it's a task requiring Christian formation.

We need to recognize that we are not immune to the centrifugal forces around us. "Everyone receives spiritual formation, just as everyone gets an education," cautioned Dallas Willard. "The only question is whether it is a good one or a bad one." All the kinds of polarization I surveyed at the end of chapter one are not just stationary obstacles to be hurdled on the path to unity; they are actively making us into persons who disdain unity. Our instinctive anxiety and suspicion of others is being hardened every day by our politics, our economy, and our media (perhaps especially the "social" kind).

If we are to avoid being "conformed to this world" (Rom 12:2), then we need actively to form each other for unity. We need to engage in practices that will help us to "in humility regard others as better than" ourselves and have "the same mind" as a Christ who "emptied himself" (Phil 2:3-7).

Start with the core practice of any Christian community: worship. If you can't quite bring yourself to share Paul and Peter's "holy kiss," make the passing of the peace a less intimate kind of icon. Sing songs that train us to listen to each other. For example, learn to sing in multipart harmony or with call and response. If you run a more contemporary service, turn down the band and let congregants hear each other! Confess your sins to one another. Make baptismal vows together. Above all else, come to the table together. Last year I asked some third graders at our church why we take Communion. God bless the boy who shot up his hand and screamed, "Because we're the body of Christ!"

Continue during the week with what might be the greatest practical legacy of the German Pietist movement: the *ecclesiola in ecclesia* ("little church within the Church"). We're more likely to join the church of Pentecost in having "all things in common" (Acts 2:44)—including opinions, questions, doubts, and anxieties—when we gather in smaller groups for study, prayer, accountability, and fellowship. We're more likely to have honest conversations about difficult issues when we converse with a few people we come to know more fully for the flawed, complicated bearers of God's image that they are.

Just keep in mind that small groups could also have the opposite effect if they become echo chambers where the like-minded gather to confirm what they already believe and deepen the grievances they already feel. Some degree of affinity is probably necessary to start these groups, but it shouldn't be too narrow—and membership should probably be somewhat fluid.

Perhaps the most important consequence of viewing Christian unity as a task of Christian formation is that we'll understand that seeking unity is a process that spans generations. For all that we ought to try to engage mature adults in practices such as those I've mentioned, it's at least as essential that churches ask themselves whether they're forming the youngest members of their congregation for unity. Whether you're a pastor, staff member, lay volunteer, or parent, consider a few big questions:

- Are you engaging children and youth in the formative practices of worship? Or are you removing them entirely from congregational gatherings—teaching them early on that the church handles diversity by segregating populations with different needs and preferences?

- As they break out into smaller groups (Sunday school classes, Wednesday night clubs, family units), are the children and youth of your church being encouraged to ask questions and share doubts? Are you helping them learn to disagree well with each other, or are you making it clear that unity is maintained by either silencing or exiling divergent opinions?

- As you place God's Word in the hands of children, are you preparing them to hold convictions courageously but also patiently and humbly?

Again, none of this is easy. But that's why we're just getting started on this topic. The next of Spener's proposals will take us even deeper into how Pietists practice Christian formation.

CHAPTER 7

Whole-Person, Whole-Life Formation

All knowledge, all learning, is dead and useless, as long as it does not impart true life to the heart, or promote the cause of practical Christianity.

Karl Wildenhahn, *Pictures from the Life of Spener*

It's time that I (Chris) confess something. I'm not actually trained as a historian of Pietism. I mostly teach classes on modern European and military/diplomatic history; my dissertation was on education in Germany after World War II. But when I came to Bethel, I heard often that it had a Pietist heritage—without also hearing a clear explanation of what that meant in practice. So I decided to put my other research on hold for a couple years and see whether I could discover a Pietist option for higher education.

Here I am, a decade later, working on my third book about Pietism.

That I came to this interest by way of education would surprise many critics of Pietism—and more than a few Pietists. From the start, other Christians have accused Pietists of feeling too much and thinking too little about their faith; some have even treated *Pietism* as another word for "anti-intellectualism." And while that's an unfair stereotype, it's not hard to find examples of Pietists regarding education with suspicion.

Early in the history of our own denomination, for example, many pietistic Covenanters refused to support anything more intellectually rigorous than a "simple preacher's school." Fortunately they were opposed by an equally devout intellectual named David Nyvall, who founded North Park University in 1891 and successfully argued that it ought to include a liberal arts curriculum. Nyvall dreamed of making the Covenant's school not just a world-class university but also a "center from which radiates to all ends of the world the light of Christ's truth, and the warmth of Christ's love, and the beauty of Christ's character." Other immigrants inspired by the Pietist ethos had similar ambitions, including Bethel's founder, John Alexis Edgren, who insisted that the Covenant's Baptist cousins needn't choose between intellectual and spiritual development.

> Coming back to Jesus makes possible the ongoing conversion and growth of the whole person throughout one's whole life.

North Park, Bethel, and several other schools founded by pietistic churches started as renewed attempts to work out something like Philipp Spener's fifth step toward securing "better times for the church": treating schools and universities as "nurseries of the church for all estates and . . . workshops of the Holy Spirit" where study and piety would be inseparable. Like Spener, Nyvall and Edgren were initially most concerned with the training of ministers, but the Pietist option for Christian formation has implications for all members of the common priesthood: laity and clergy, young and old. It makes clear that Christianity is indeed more than we think because coming back to Jesus makes possible the ongoing conversion and growth of the whole person throughout one's whole life, to God's glory and our neighbors' good.

A Pietist Vision for Christian Higher Education—and Beyond

In 2015 I had the privilege of editing a collection of essays by current and former Bethel colleagues titled *The Pietist Vision of Christian Higher Education: Forming Whole and Holy Persons*. While our focus was squarely on Christian colleges such as Bethel and North Park, much of what we shared is relevant for Christian formation at other stages of life, from young children learning in Sunday school to mature adults training for ministry and leadership in seminary.

So in the first half of this chapter I'll identify three major themes of our Pietist vision for higher education. Then I'll conclude by starting to think through how those principles might be applied in other settings.

The Jesus-centered college. Evangelicals in higher education often use the term *Christ-centered* to distinguish their colleges and universities from those that maintain some historic tie to a denomination but are only nominally Christian. I value Bethel's distinctively Christian curriculum and community, but I think Pietists would be more likely to say that education ought to be "Jesus-centered."

Don't get me wrong: I believe that Jesus is the Christ, and Christian formation at any level should seek to work out the implications of that theological claim for our learning and living. But I've always been struck by Phyllis Tickle's observation that Pietism gave evangelicalism "its great comfort with 'Jesus' talk. It's probably not an exaggeration to say that while 'Christ' was central to Pietism, 'Jesus' as a name or term for Messiah, by virtue of being more personal, was more central." So even in an academic setting, Pietism reminds us that the center of our lived faith is not an idea (however true) but a person.

> Pietism reminds us that the center of our lived faith is not an idea (however true) but a person.

That point is central to the way Bethel's longest-serving president thought about higher education. In 1959 Carl Lundquist explained that "the unifying center of [Bethel's] academic program is neither Truth nor the Pursuit of Truth but is Jesus Christ Himself. Ultimately, in our Christian view, Truth and Christ are one, and the important thing about Truth is that it ought to point to Christ." Eleven years later, with the campus divided by the Vietnam War, Lundquist located Bethel's first "point of unity" in a common personal commitment to Jesus: "He has become the supreme affection in our lives. As a result we enjoy a personal and intimate relationship with the Lord that adds the warm overtones of deep spiritual devotion to all of life."

Similarly, when Covenant scholar Karl Olsson was appointed president of his denomination's college and seminary in 1959, he celebrated that "the faith which underlies the intellectual process at North Park . . . is articulated in a personal encounter with Jesus Christ." An education centered on that encounter, he told North Park faculty two years later, "is primarily interested in pointing beyond itself and beyond all created things to the Source of life and truth, who by giving . . . Himself to us sustains within us the hunger for salvation." In *The Pietist Vision of Christian Higher Education*, my favorite version of what Olsson described came from Dick Peterson, a physicist who grew up in the Covenant Church: "The modern scientist of pietistic background and faith will often find the personal experience of research bringing them closer to their Creator. . . . Astonishment is no small deal in science, and the nineteenth Psalm [e.g., Ps 19:1-4] affirms that such an encounter with the transcendent is marvelously complementary to our more rational embrace of God's laws."

"In the uncertain and perhaps bizarre pilgrimage on which you enter," Olsson told North Park graduates in 1965, "we leave you in the care of a *person*. Not of a system of values or of an intuition or even of a revelation but of the word made flesh and living in our midst." Whatever else I have to say in this chapter, know that the Pietist option for Christian formation, at any level, starts and ends with the Alpha and Omega, Jesus, who is not only the truth but the way and the life (Jn 14:6).

Transformation, not just information. Precisely because it "begins with the experience of knowing Jesus Christ personally," says former Bethel theology professor Roger Olson, a Pietist "model of Christian higher education values *transformation* over *information* without discarding or demeaning information and critical thinking." If they attend such a college or university and experience such encounters, students should expect to receive more than job training. They should find themselves changed from the inside out, with "all of life and thought centered consistently around the person of Jesus Christ: his love, his justice, his peace, his care of persons."

In short, we're talking about education as conversion. Christian formation helps turn us back to Jesus—and turns us into persons more like Jesus. According to Karl Olsson, the student's encounter with Jesus "endows his existence with a new quality. He views existence from a new perspective." *New* is the key word there: having been given new birth, we must learn how to live the new life as new creatures in a world that is itself being made new.

Even in an academic setting Christian formation is not simply about changing our minds. Even for a philosopher such as David Williams, encountering Jesus at a school like Bethel "will leave one altered in all senses of what it means to be a person." We aspire to form *whole and holy persons* who "love the Lord your God . . . with all your mind" but also "with all your heart, and with all your soul . . . and with all your strength" (Mk 12:30). Similarly, at North Park Olsson insisted that "education is linked not only to the training of the intellect but to the salvation of *the whole man*."

If seeing the word *conversion* made you think of what Mark wrote in chapter five, seeing *whole* might remind you of what I wrote in chapter six. In education as much as any other realm, the mission is the same: what was broken is being made whole; what was sick is being healed. Indeed, the language of healing and wholeness recurs throughout *Pietist Vision*. Williams observes that "when one's whole person is involved [in learning], one experiences a kind of movement analogous to the movement *from sickness to health*." Roger Olson sums up the Pietist purpose of education in this way: "to glorify God and form persons in God's image—that is, *to heal and make whole* God's image in them."

> In education, the mission is the same: what was broken is being made whole; what was sick is being healed.

Education in community, for communities. Because of its emphasis on the personal experience of conversion, Pietism has sometimes been criticized for promoting religious individualism. Tellingly, though, there was scarcely any chapter in our 2015 book that didn't emphasize the importance of community—both as a means and an end—for the Pietist vision of education.

For example, after conversion, the second theme running through David Williams's chapter is the Pietist yearning for the closer, more authentically Christian community that one experiences within the *ecclesiola*. Psychologist Kathy Nevins develops that idea in the next chapter:

> What Pietists advocated, and contemporary research and practice supports, is that cultivating Christian maturity is best done in community. In community, students (and faculty) are able to encounter the challenges necessary for growth and to receive the supports needed to meet those challenges. The classroom becomes what [Ray] Oldenburg called a "third place," where one is known, feels safe and can engage with others in ways that expand one's understanding of self, others, the world and God—that is, the pietistic pursuit of wholeness and holiness.

For Nevins, the small-group-like community of the classroom is what makes possible the formation of whole and holy persons.

For it's not just individual wholeness or holiness that we're after. Through such a learning community, Nevins continues, "all will sense the connections that convey the ethic of care and love for neighbor." Again and again the book suggests that the marks of holiness include humility, open-mindedness, hospitality, and love—the virtues most necessary for Christians living in a pluralistic society. Likewise, the mark of wholeness is personal integrity lived out in service to a broken world. Like our Jesuit cousins, Pietist educators form "men and women *for others*."

Nowhere is that point made more clearly than in Sara Shady and Marion Larson's call for Christian college professors and students to engage in interfaith dialogue and service. Inspired by Gary Sattler's observation that for A. H. Francke "faith was a verb," Shady and Larson felt "a responsibility to extend learning beyond mere intellectual activity to actual engagement with the people living beyond the borders of our campuses." By arranging on-campus forums and off-campus service projects with Muslims and other non-Christians, Larson, Shady, and colleagues such as historian Amy Poppinga have helped Bethel students "learn firsthand lessons about how to live out the Christian responsibility of hospitality: to welcome the stranger in their midst and to love the neighbor who is different from their usual neighbors."

A Pietist Vision for Children, Youth, and Family Ministry?

Hear, O Israel: The LORD is our God, the LORD alone. You shall love the LORD your God with all your heart, and with all your soul, and with all your might. Keep these words that I am commanding you today in your heart. Recite them to your children and talk about them when you are at home and when you are away, when you lie down and when you rise.

DEUTERONOMY 6:4-7

In his influential book *Desiring the Kingdom*, Reformed philosopher James K. A. Smith suggests that some Christian colleges avoid the language of Christian formation "because such talk seems to come with the baggage of fundamentalist pietism. It seems to make the Christian college an extension of Sunday school." For a long time, that was my least favorite passage in my favorite book on Christian formation—one more misbegotten example of how Pietism is casually dismissed as a kind of anti-intellectualism. But I've come to read those lines differently. Perhaps what we do in higher education *is* an extension of the formation that starts with programs such as Sunday school. And perhaps the principles we identified with Pietist colleges and universities such as Bethel in *Pietist Vision* could benefit Christians at earlier stages of their spiritual, intellectual, and emotional development.

When I first started researching Pietism and education, my children hadn't yet been born. Now not only am I the father of twin second graders, but I've had chances to work with everyone from preschoolers to teenagers in our church's Sunday morning, Wednesday evening, and summer programs. So I increasingly wonder how our Pietist vision for later stages of education would apply to the Christian formation of children and adolescents. I don't have any firm conclusions here, but I think the Pietist option opens three questions that might provoke fruitful conversation among parents and those who work in children, youth, and family ministry.

Does formation take place in community for the sake of the larger community? He was speaking about higher education, but Carl Lundquist's words seem pertinent here as well: "In the end the impact of one life upon another is probably greater than the impact of an idea or a method of teaching or a favorable physical setting." It's not that we don't want thoughtful curriculum or inviting facilities for this kind of ministry, but it's essential that meaningful relationships form among students, teachers, mentors, parents, and pastors. It's especially important that such learning communities be intergenerational. Faith will be "stickier," researchers at Fuller Seminary have found, if children and teenagers get to know well five adults at church other than their parents.

Just remember that "the only thing that counts is faith working through love" (Gal 5:6). The community that takes shape within the church must reach out to other communities if it is to form young persons in the likeness of Christ the Servant of Culture. Our kids love being at church, but their most formative experience came away from it: when we joined other families in packing meals at a Christian ministry called Feed My Starving Children (FMSC). As they worked with other kids to fill bag after bag with rice, soy, and dried vegetables, Lena and Isaiah learned (in the words of FMSC's theme verse) that the Lord "upholds the cause of the oppressed and gives food to the hungry" (Ps 146:7 NIV).

Are you seeking to form the whole person, even early in life? A couple of years ago, a parents' group at our church was reading through Valerie Hess and Marti Watson Garlett's book *Habits of a Child's Heart: Raising Your Kids with the Spiritual Disciplines.* So my wife and I decided to try out a few of Hess and Garlett's suggestions with our fourth-grade Sunday school class. For a month we spent time talking about prayer, meditation and silence, study, and service—their roots in Jesus' life and other biblical examples and how nine- and ten-year-olds might practice them. It was a good reminder to us that we were not simply filling young minds with biblical facts and quotations but helping to make disciples—

disciplined followers of Jesus Christ who seek to love God with their souls as well as their hearts and minds.

Most importantly, is Christian formation centered on the person of Jesus Christ? In the end, there is no "impact of one life upon another" greater than the impact of Jesus' life upon the lives of young people. "Let the little children come to me," Jesus told his disciples, "and do not stop them; for it is to such as these that the kingdom of heaven belongs" (Mt 19:14). But anyone who has worked in children, youth, or family ministry knows that the (good) means to that end can sometimes get in the way. Precisely because we're so eager to have the best possible programming, scheduling, curriculum, volunteer training, and so on, it's possible that any or all of those (again, good) things can actually divert our attention from Jesus himself.

That diversion might even be true of how we present the Bible. On the one hand, any Pietist would say that it's imperative to put God's written Word in the hands of children. Since the Scriptures, said Spener, "are the letter of the heavenly Father to all his children, no child of God can be excluded from them, but all have both the right and the command to read them (John 5:38)." But David Nyvall warned that "it is possible to believe the Bible *instead* of believing in God. The worst way to lose the Bible is to make it into an idol." We can be so concerned with cultivating biblical literacy—memorizing verses! sword drills!—that the Bible becomes the center of our ministry, not Jesus.

Once more, we need to reject the idea that we face an either-or choice: the Bible or Jesus. The former, said Martin Luther, is the cradle where we find the latter. "Pietists loved the Bible," write Roger Olson and Christian Collins Winn, "because it is the principal medium for the Christian's relationship with God, helping to guide and develop a deep and genuine intimacy between the Christian and God."

But think back to the problems that Mark identified in chapter three. If we've lost sight of the truly transformative power of God's Word, perhaps it's because we've inculcated some bad habits early on in the lives of those who read it. Are you making the Bible seem like a collection of information to be filed away, or are you helping children and youth approach the Scriptures prayerfully and reverently, as that "altar where we meeting the living God"? Are you reading the Bible so that the little children come to Jesus, or do those young disciples think that *it*, and not Jesus, is the center of their faith?

What About Seminaries?

The three questions just listed are all good questions for the Christian formation of adults as well, but let me close by thinking aloud about how Pietists would approach the education of one particular group of more mature Christians: future pastors and others called to work in churches.

After all, the training of ministers was Spener's original focus in *Pia Desideria*'s fifth proposal. And before it added a college, Bethel was simply the Swedish Baptist Seminary, whose founder wanted students to "be conscious of a real conversion and a call to the gospel ministry." Echoing Spener, John Alexis Edgren emphasized that the seminary educated the whole person: "Thus, while storing the mind with useful information of a biblical as well as a secular nature, spiritual edification must never be lost sight of." Moreover, this kind of holistic formation happened primarily via a student-professor relationship marked by "real friendship and helpfulness, remembering that One is our Master, and we are all brethren."

Roger Olson reports that when he moved from teaching college students at Bethel to teaching future pastors at Baylor University, he found the Pietist ethos in both settings. In particular, he noted Truett Seminary's emphasis on learning in a Jesus-centered community:

> At the center of everything about the seminary is Jesus Christ and personal experience of his living, transforming presence. Professors as well as students meet weekly for hour-long "covenant group" meetings in which we practice *lectio divina* and pray for one another, our community, and the world. In my covenant group we sing hymns and tell stories of our personal journeys.

Edgren's emphasis on "spiritual edification" can also be found in the history of North Park. Under the leadership of theologian John Weborg, a scholar of Pietism, North Park Seminary began to incorporate spiritual formation into its curriculum in the late 1970s. North Park has since added a center for the training of spiritual directors, named for Weborg.

This is not to say theological education shouldn't provide excellent training in, well, theology. But there is a distinctive way that Pietists think about God. Insisting that intellectual study is only "a servant of God's main purpose, which is to transform us into Christ-like persons," Collins Winn and Olson describe Pietist theology as being "guided (not governed) by prayer and devotion. Pietism believes that Christian theology should never be a merely academic exercise; it should be practiced and believed within the bosom of the worshiping community by individuals whose lives are committed to Christ by faith." Such theology must also make room for honest doubt and disagreement. "It is imperative that faith, if it be living faith," wrote North Park Seminary dean Don Frisk in 1963, "raise questions about itself and face honestly the questions which others raise."

Finally, while a Pietist seminary ought to seek the intellectual breadth and depth that David Nyvall intended for North Park, it should also take seriously the concern at the core of his opponents' preference for a "simple preacher's school." For no part of the pastor's calling is more important than his or her ability to proclaim the gospel. But I'll let my coauthor—one of the best preachers I know—tell you more about our final proposal for the renewal of the church.

CHAPTER 8

Proclaiming the Good News

"Everyone who calls on the name of the Lord shall be saved."

*But how are they to call on one in whom they have not be-
lieved? And how are they to believe in one of whom they have
never heard? And how are they to hear without someone to
proclaim him? And how are they to proclaim him unless they
are sent? As it is written, "How beautiful are the feet of those
who bring good news!"*

Romans 10:13-15

Philipp Spener's sixth and final proposal for improving the conditions of the church was "that sermons be so prepared by all that
their purpose (faith and its fruits) may be achieved in the hearers to the
greatest possible degree." In our day, this goal remains crucial for pastors
like me (Mark), yet Spener's proposal needs to be purposefully
broadened to the many and varied ways the good news of God's love is
proclaimed. Those in our churches and society today do not look solely
to the clergy for a word from God, if they look to them at all. A more
hopeful future for the church and the world must include a renewal in
our preaching, but more than ever it must also extend to the other
forms of proclamation to which God calls all of us.

Much has been made, and with good reason, of the quotation supposedly uttered by St. Francis of Assisi: "Preach the gospel at all times.

When necessary, use words." The truth is, though, that it is unlikely Francis said it. Certainly his lifestyle and actions were consistent with the gospel of Jesus, but the up to five sermons he preached each day in village after village indicate that he thought the words of the gospel were extremely important too. When it comes to following Jesus' call in our lives and sharing the life-giving Word of God with others, we must again avoid the dichotomy of either-or thinking. We must give ourselves fully to the task with both our actions and our words.

As we look at the ministry of preaching and something we are calling a ministry of listening, we especially want to encourage and even challenge the church to take up our God-given ministry of evangelism. By this we mean sharing the saving Word of God with both those outside the church and those within it. We are talking about doing so with both our actions and our words, with the kind of loving fervor that can only happen as we share with others that which has made a difference in our own lives.

This indeed is the critical factor in our proclamation of the gospel. We must be experiencing it ourselves as good news if we hope to share it as such.

A Ministry of Preaching

Many a beautiful sermon containing wonderful truth and dressed in eloquent language falls to the ground like a bird shot down in flight. What is lacking? No heart! Nothing is wrong with its theology. The teaching is correct, and the truth is spoken. Scripture after Scripture is quoted. The presentation is quiet and orderly, and the language is dignified and stately. Despite all this, not a soul is gripped by the message.

GUSTAF F. JOHNSON

Why do so many well-written, theologically correct, Bible-quoting sermons fall flat to the ground? "Simply," answered the Swedish-American preacher Gustaf Johnson, "because the preacher has neglected to make what he says a vital issue for himself." For those in the common priesthood called to preach, proclaiming the Word of God must begin with listening to the Word of God. We must—as we hope those who hear us will—allow it "to penetrate to the heart." We are called not just to read words printed in our Bibles or to reflect on words of wisdom about the Word of God gleaned from other great thinkers and spiritual giants. We who hope to share the Word of God with others must first invite, allow, and expect God to speak his Word to us.

This is holy work, work that we hope all Christians will do if they wish to share the good news of God's Word with others. But it's absolutely essential that those of us who preach take up this work.

Spener acknowledged that there were more than enough sermons being preached to late seventeenth-century Germans. He grieved, though, that too many were aimed at showcasing the abilities of the preacher rather than "plainly but powerfully" proclaiming the Word of God. The sermon should serve as "the divine means to save people," he urged. It should be understood as sacramental in nature, in the sense that God is present and graciously at work in the preaching and the listening. Sermons are vehicles through which God can work to awaken people to God's great love and the new life in Christ in which love of God and neighbor overflows.

> We who hope to share the Word of God with others must first invite, allow, and expect God to speak his Word to us.

True transformation, Spener argued, takes place from the inside out, so he urged preachers to aim their sermons toward the "inner man or the new man, whose soul is faith and whose expressions are the fruit of life." Outward actions not arising from the fertile soil of a vibrant inner life are soon burned away by the heat of trial and testing or choked out by the cares, riches, and pleasures of life (see Lk 8:4-15). Both preachers and listeners must be aware that "it is not enough that we hear the Word with our outward ear, but we must let it penetrate to our heart, so that we may hear the Holy Spirit speak there, that is, with vibrant emotion and comfort feel the sealing of the Spirit and the power of the Word."

For Pietists, all that we do in life and ministry, including our preaching, is to be done with the prayer that God would transform people's hearts, minds, and lives. This transforming work is something only God can do, though by God's grace we gladly participate in it. Trying to do this great work in our own wisdom and power only leads us, again and again, to produce the "works of the flesh" (Gal 5:19), what Spener called "mere hypocrisy." Our great need is that the inner person be so strengthened to trust God's promises that we allow Christ's Spirit to bring forth his fruit among us. As we do, by God's great power and to his glory, we find ourselves accomplishing "abundantly far more than all we can ask or imagine" (Eph 3:20).

For the pastor, expectant faith is what we must bring not only to our preaching but to our sermon preparation, our personal devotional times, and all we do. It is a faith that is needed not only when we stand in the pulpit but whenever we open up the Scriptures or kneel down to pray. In this we lead the way in inviting every member of Christ's body to practice living all of life in the transformative presence of God. Preparing to preach or preaching, preparing to serve or serving—in all that we do and invite others to do, we do it before God with a sense of wonder and hope. We trust that God is with us, speaks to us, empowers us, guides us, is at work within and around us. We come before God in faith, our senses alert and our spirits eager to join in with the gracious work of the Holy Spirit in us, the church, and the world.

The need for such faith seems more apparent than ever as we look at the fractured, angry, and increasingly rigid battle lines so evident in society, the church, and even many families. Sharing the words that communicate the gospel is essential, but the reality is that long before they can be heard, a certain softening of the heart and opening of the mind is needed. It may be that one of the most powerful ways we in the common priesthood can participate in the work of God in the lives of others—and likely open ourselves up to that work as well—is through the humble, loving act of listening. And here we Pietists must hear the voices of some other Christians.

A Ministry of Listening

You must understand this, my beloved: let everyone be quick to listen, slow to speak, slow to anger; for your anger does not produce God's righteousness.

JAMES 1:19-20

"Not everything has to be a culture war," pleaded Caleb Kaltenbach in 2015. Lead pastor of a nondenominational church near Los Angeles and author of *Messy Grace: How a Pastor with Gay Parents Learned to Love Others Without Sacrificing Conviction*, Kaltenbach had arranged a meeting at Biola University between gay Christian activist Matthew Vines and leading conservatives, including radio host Frank Sontag and author and speaker Sean McDowell. That conversation convinced Kaltenbach "all the more that evangelical Christians need to do more listening than talking right now."

Another evangelical pastor told me that he heard trusted friends making the same point the previous summer as he wrestled with how to relate to his son, who self-identified as gay. "Shut up and just listen," his friends bluntly put it. "He already knows how you feel about this." A year later their relationship has been transformed. "I have the most fantastic relationship with my son!" the pastor recently exclaimed. His views haven't changed, nor has his son come to share them, but as he told us, "My son's being drawn by love to the King. He's attending church, thinking about joining a small group, and although he's not settled on this issue, he wants to be faithful. He called just last week to tell me, 'God's really moving in my life!'"

How did these transformations come about in the pastor's relationship with his son and his son's relationship with God? Clearly, his first answer is "The grace of God!" But he is quick to add, "I stopped talking, stopped trying to be the Holy Spirit's voice, and started being quiet and just listening."

That commitment to listening has not only transformed his relationship with his son, but it has tempered his tendency to play what he called the "angry prophet" with his congregation. In short, the pastor has discovered the calling that religion journalist Krista Tippett once described for *Christianity Today*. "There's absolutely ministry in it," she said of her public radio conversation series, *On Being*. "It's simply a ministry of listening rather than of preaching."

Yet Christians, warned Dietrich Bonhoeffer in his 1939 classic, *Life Together*, "so often think they must always contribute something when they are in the company of others, that this is the one service they have to render. They forget that listening can be a greater service than speaking." How much worse that problem when so many of our relationships are largely virtual. In an age of social media, we feel always "in the company of others" and may often imagine that the best thing we have to offer—possibly the thing we have a responsibility to offer—is our voice (or tweet, blog post, or Facebook status update).

"Many people are looking for an ear that will listen," wrote Bonhoeffer. He was writing at the eve of World War II, but he could have been describing our day. "They do not find it among Christians, because these Christians are talking where they should be listening." In a lonely society, to listen is to love. And in a polarized society, to listen is to offer a winsome witness.

> In a lonely society, to listen is to love. And in a polarized society, to listen is to offer a winsome witness.

The Catholic novelist Flannery O'Connor once explained that she penned such startling, sometimes grotesque stories because when an author writes for an audience that doesn't share her beliefs, "you have to make your vision apparent by shock—to the hard of hearing you shout." But today, with the cacophony of voices clamoring for attention, if we want to shock those who don't share our beliefs, we may need to do the reverse. We may need to listen to them.

Certainly this is what caught the attention of the pastor's son. When the son took his father up on an offer to help him move across the country, the dad dedicated himself to "being quiet and kind. If he brought up homosexuality, I didn't start preaching. I asked myself, 'How would the prodigal's father treat him?' and kept in mind that without my Heavenly Father's mercy toward me, 'I'd be toast.'" He was generous to his son, not overdoing it but seeking "to love him wisely."

At their last dinner together, on a Saturday evening, he focused once again on listening and then enjoyed seeing the conversation develop into a joint sharing of life experiences.

"Dad, now I know you really love me," his son exclaimed after a while. "I've always loved you, son," the pastor replied.

While we should have the humility to admit that we have something to learn from any conversation, we need not silence our consciences to listen to others. Neither the father nor the son changed his mind that evening or, as of this writing, since. But committing to a ministry of listening should leave us less eager to win an argument than to sustain a relationship.

There are no guarantees as to what others will choose to do when we choose to listen, any more than there are when we choose to speak. But we can take up a ministry of listening in the hope that it is through such choices that God brings reconciliation and peace into the tumult of our times. "It is God's love for us," wrote Bonhoeffer, "that He not only gives us His Word but also lends us His ear. So it is His work that we do for our brother when we learn to listen to him."

A Ministry of Going to the World

But you will receive power when the Holy Spirit has come upon you; and you will be my witnesses in Jerusalem, in all Judea and Samaria, and to the ends of the earth.

ACTS 1:8

At the end of the Gospel of Luke, Jesus tells his disciples "that the Messiah is to suffer and rise from the dead on the third day, and that repentance and forgiveness of sins is to be proclaimed in his name to all nations" (Lk 24:46-47). In a very real way he's telling them that he's fulfilled his part of the biblical prophecy through his death and resurrection, and now it is time for them to do their part in proclaiming this good news. As in John 20:21, where Jesus states, "As the Father has sent me, so I send you," the message following the resurrection sounds a lot like "Tag, you're it!" In other words, "Now it's your turn. Your turn to share my peace with the world. Love others as I have loved you. Call people to repentance, inviting them to turn like the prodigal toward home and the life they were created to live. Go into all the world and offer the good news of forgiveness of sins, calling people to come, allow themselves to be loved, and receive the new life God longs to give to all."

Tag, we're it. We are the ones who have been graced with the joyful privilege and astounding responsibility to serve as Christ's witnesses to the world. Empowered by Christ's Spirit, this task has taken Jesus' followers as near as the neighborhoods where they lived and as far as the most distant corners of the globe. For example, August Hermann Francke's ministry in Halle, Germany, both provided care and education for local children and trained the first Protestant missionaries to India. But whether Jesus' call leads us down the block or to "the ends of the earth," his example compels us to not only speak of the good news but to live it out: to give ourselves in love for our neighbors, to build relationships with them, to listen to their joys and sorrows, and to invite them to experience God's life-giving grace. As Bonhoeffer suggests, we do well to pattern our loving of others on what we experience in God's loving of us.

This love we see in God and are called to practice ourselves is one that is continually reaching out, pursuing us, and calling us home. It reminds me in a small way of when I was young and our little beagle, Daisy, would occasionally wander away. As soon as someone realized she was missing, the call to action was sounded. No matter what we were up to, everyone joined in, afraid that she might get lost or hit by a car. It was a family affair: going out through the streets, calling her name, doing all we could to bring her home.

Jesus told similar stories to explain his behavior when criticized for spending time with tax collectors and sinners. Through images of lost sheep, lost coins, and lost sons, Jesus made it clear that seeking those who were lost was what he was about (Lk 15). Like the prodigal son and the brother who resented him, we are prone to squander our inheritance, reject our Father's love, and wander far from home. And like them we find ourselves day by day, again and again, invited by our heavenly Father to come to the table and to bring with us all those we can.

But our evangelistic efforts can be as ineffective as the work of the preacher whose sermon falls like a bird downed in mid-flight. To the degree this is true, it is because we are not coming to the table ourselves, drinking of the new wine and eating of the fresh bread laid before us each day. We are trying to pass on a thing that is not living and active for us—not now, anyway, not anymore. We are attempting to share a new life that we are not experiencing ourselves. Covenant pastor Glen Wiberg described the problem—and the solution—in this way:

> Growing up in church, I heard a lot of testimonies about conversion that occurred twenty-five years earlier. The same recital week after week. Nothing current in thin places since they had become ossified—meaning rigid, conventional, opposed to change. You can escape ossification only by a fresh encounter with God, a fresh dip in the waters of your baptism, a being born again and again.

What our proclamation of the good news needs, whether in a sermon or a testimony, over a coffee table, at work, or in the backyard, is the fire of a life alive, growing, and overflowing in the abounding grace of God's Spirit and Word. We too must come again and again back to Jesus, back to the party, back to eat and drink at the table. And as we go, we will discover that it makes all the sense in heaven and on earth to invite yet others to join us as well.

> What our proclamation of the good news needs is the fire of a life alive, growing, and overflowing.

"Evangelism is the spontaneous expression of abundant life in Christ," wrote another influential Covenant pastor, Wesley Nelson. "It is a quality of life that flows out to the world around which, in the power of the holy Spirit, convinces other people to believe also." The ways this abundant life can flow out of us into the world around are numerous. Our outreach includes our actions, our service, and our efforts in working for justice, mercy, and peace for all. Yet it also includes our personal words and our sharing of God's transformative Word. Our outreach may well include personal invitations to church events and services, but it must also include sharing our stories and where Christ's story connects with and transforms them.

Our outreach may include participating in church-sponsored pro-grams, going on mission trips, and even following God's call into a vocation of missions nationally or abroad. Yet for all of us it must in-clude praying that God would open our eyes with love to those around us and give us the courage to step out in faith in response to Jesus' Great Commission (Mt 28:18-20). This is a family affair. We are all in this together until all are present with us at God's table of grace, expe-riencing God's goodness, glory, and love.

Forward in Faith, Hope, and Love

"How goes your walk?" Swedish Pietists often asked. It is not the kind of question that invites us to make a distinction between those who are in and those who are out. It rather points toward a way—*the Way*—forward for us all. It invites us to take our next step of faith, wherever we are or have been, and to encourage others to do the same. Thinking back to my walk in the desert that I mentioned in chapter five, it is a question that encourages us to rejoice that Jesus invites us to walk with him, follow him, and venture forward with him to learn, live, and serve to-gether in his name.

God's kingdom is near, breaking into our world with the same power that raised Jesus Christ from the dead. Remarkably, God has given us the joyful privilege of joining together with his Spirit and church in that mighty work. Every time I consider that it is people like us through whom Jesus chooses to make this plan of God work, I am stunned. I can't help but notice that when he announced his Great Commission, Jesus didn't wait until all of his disciples' doubts and questions had been resolved. He didn't wait until their theology was in order. He didn't wait until they wouldn't make mistakes, embarrass him or one another, or let him or each other down. He just said, "Go!" and "I am with you!" and sent them out to participate in the gracious work of God in the world.

We are called to pray in the belief that God gives "the Holy Spirit to those who ask him" (Lk 11:13). We are called to faithful acts of obedience, believing, as Ananias did, that God works through even those actions that seem of little value or of great risk (Acts 9:10-19). We are called to boldly preach, believing with Peter that God is able to "cut to the heart" as the Word is proclaimed (Acts 2:37) and pour out the Holy Spirit on those who are listening (Acts 10:34-48).

Jesus is on the move, and he calls us to go with him. With all of our weaknesses and our stumbling, our uncertainties and our doubts, he calls us to venture forward with him, announcing the good news of God's kingdom and participating in making its transforming presence known on earth. Forward we go, sharing the grace of God, encouraging one another, and inviting yet others to join with Jesus in this joyful walk of faith, hope, and love.

Benediction

"Like a Tree Planted by Water"

Outside the window of my (Mark's) study, there's an oak tree that towers over the church lawn. Its branches stretch upward and outward in every direction. Its roots, unseen, run deep and wide. Its beginning took place, against all odds, long before my arrival. Its vitality is likely to continue long after I'm gone—blessing the hungry squirrels, offering a resting place for birds, providing shade and truckloads of leaves for our church's preschool children to laugh and play in.

I've continued a tradition of watering the tree, doing my little part. It started with our late friend Glen Wiberg, who pastored Salem Covenant Church in the 1980s and died while we were completing revisions on this book. After worship services are over, following Glen's example the pastors often bring the water left in the baptismal font out to the tree. With the help of children whenever possible, we pour the water at the base of the trunk.

As we do, I feel a sense of connection to the past, the future, and the ongoing gracious work of God. I think of the tree and give thanks for this moment from its long lifespan that I share. I think of the sacrament of baptism and its waters that are in view so briefly and then quickly gone from sight. I think of how the life of the one baptized will continue: the baptismal waters, though unseen, forever a part of the fabric of the person's identity and being.

We, like those who have gone before us, are only here for a while. This is our chance to do our little part, to make our meager offering of love to God and neighbor amid the changing seasons of our world. The offerings of our predecessors, including those of the Pietists to whom we have looked, were not perfect. Our offerings won't be either. Yet like them we offer ourselves with gratitude for the privilege.

The church is alive, against all odds, because of the grace of God. The church continues to stand through all the tempests and troubles, both from within and without, because of the grace of God. We can hope for better times not because we have come to believe that our human wisdom, power, or righteousness will somehow suddenly be sufficient. We are people of hope because we believe God's grace is far more than sufficient.

In Jeremiah we read that "those who trust in the LORD . . . shall be like a tree planted by water, sending out its roots by the stream." In contrast, "those who trust in mere mortals . . . shall be like a shrub in the desert, and shall not see when relief comes" (Jer 17:5-8). Practically speaking, both groups of people are located in the same spot. By faith one is able to see and be nourished by the gift of God's grace; the other is blind to it. Like the people of Jeremiah's time, like Spener and later Pietists, we face challenges that can seem overwhelming. Like them we also have the opportunity to be a part of what God can do in and through us, even beyond what we dream.

God's great river of grace runs close by, as close as our very breath and even closer. Stretching out our roots into that river, venturing upward and outward in faith and hope, may we bear the good fruit of God's love in the world, to God's glory and our neighbor's good. In the name of the Father, and of the Son, and of the Holy Spirit. Amen.

Now to him who by the power at work within us is able to accomplish abundantly far more than all we can ask or imagine, to him be glory in the church and in Christ Jesus to all generations, forever and ever. Amen. (Eph 3:20-21)

Appendix

Learn More About Pietism

If you'd like to learn more about the historical roots of the Pietist option, the best place to begin is Roger Olson and Christian Collins Winn's *Reclaiming Pietism: Retrieving an Evangelical Tradition*, which starts with familiar figures such as Spener, Francke, and Zinzendorf but then follows the Pietist ethos into the nineteenth and twentieth centuries. Other good, brief, affordable introductions to the German Pietist movement are Dale Brown's *Understanding Pietism* and Michelle Clifton-Soderstrom's *Angels, Worms, and Bogeys*. For biographies, see K. James Stein on Spener, Gary Sattler on Francke, and Barbara Becker-Cantarino on Johanna Petersen.

As a field of academic research, Pietism studies has taken off of late in both Europe and North America. Canadian scholar Douglas Shantz's *Introduction to German Pietism* will bring you up to speed. See also the wide-ranging collection *The Pietist Impulse in Christianity*, which Chris helped to edit.

If our many references to our denomination have made you curious about the history of the Evangelical Covenant Church, a wide variety of primary and secondary sources are available online in the Donald Frisk Collection of Covenant Literature (collections.carli.illinois.edu /cdm/landingpage/collection/npu_swecc). And it's more than half a century old now, but Karl Olsson's *By One Spirit* is both an important denominational history and an argument for the influence of Pietism on Covenanters.

We haven't said quite as much about Bethel University or its denomination, Converge Worldwide, but Chris's *Pietist Vision of Christian Higher Education* and the online issues of the *Baptist Pietist Clarion* (baptistpietistclarion.com) will help you understand how the Pietist ethos has shaped those institutions.

The biennial journal *Pietisten* (pietisten.org) features writings drawn from the Evangelical Covenant Church, Converge, and other denominational descendants of the nineteenth-century Pietist revival in Sweden. Its editor, Mark Safstrom, recently published *The Swedish Pietists*, featuring his translations of writings and sermons by C. O. Rosenius (editor of the original *Pietisten*) and his successor, P. P. Waldenström. For a broader survey of Pietism in that part of the world, see Lutheran historian Mark Granquist's *Scandinavian Pietists*.

Using This Book
for Personal Devotions or
Small Group Discussion

E ver since the days of Philipp Spener and Johanna Petersen, Pietists have been committed to devotional practices, both by individuals and within small groups. So we've written *The Pietist Option* in the hope that it can be integrated into your private devotions and become a useful resource for small groups.

To facilitate both individual reflection and small group discussion, we've suggested some questions for each chapter. But we'd also encourage you to integrate your reading of this book with your ongoing study of Scripture. For indeed Spener was right: "The more at home the Word of God is among us, the more we shall bring about faith and its fruits."

Before you read each chapter or before your small group discusses it, try applying Mark's PRAY acronym to the biblical passages suggested:

- **Pray:** Come to the Bible in prayer. Submit yourself to God, invite the Holy Spirit to enlighten you, and ask God to speak to you and enable you to live according to God's gracious purpose.

- **Repent:** Turn toward God and let God love you, guide you, and have his way with you. Open yourself in humility and trust our Father's love as you meet him at the altar of his holy Word.

- **Ask:** Come to the Scriptures asking questions of God and of yourself. Be curious, expectant, imaginative, open, and interested in seeing what you haven't yet seen, understanding what you haven't yet understood, appreciating what you haven't yet appreciated. Ask others to help you listen to the Scriptures, understand them, wrestle with them, and live them. Don't try to listen to God solely on your own.

- **Yes:** Come to the Scriptures to say yes to God: "Yes, I want to allow you to love me. Yes, I want to receive the nourishment, guidance, transformation, and empowerment you offer. Yes, I want to love you with all of my heart, soul, mind, and strength, and my neighbor as myself. Yes, I want your will to be done in and through me."

For more about the PRAY method, see pages 50-55.

Introduction: "Come Back to Jesus"

PRAY passage: John 14:1-7

1. The introduction ends with a question that the Pietists of Mark's and Chris's experience have often asked each other: "How goes your walk with Christ?" How would you answer that question yourself? (If you're in a small group, you might start your time together by sharing stories of your walk with Christ.)

2. Have you heard of Pietism before? In what context? Before reading this introduction, how would you have explained Pietism to someone else?

3. Which of the four Pietist instincts resonates most strongly with you?

4. Mark and Chris are writing as longtime members of the Evangelical Covenant Church, perhaps the most explicitly Pietist denomination in America. How important is denominational identity or religious tradition to you? If you don't come from an especially Pietist background, how might Pietism "leaven" your experience of Christianity?

Chapter 1: What's Wrong?

PRAY passage: Jeremiah 9:1-6

1. Before you get too far into this chapter, pause to pray. Ask God the questions that Chris asked himself while writing: "What's your word

for me? And then what's your word *through me?* What can I share with others that may be helpful, by the grace of your Spirit?"

2. In what circumstances do you act like God is absent even though you believe in God? What kind of things can make you feel like a "functional atheist"?

3. Have you experienced that "the same people who argue most strenuously for the historicity of the resurrection can seem like the least likely to live as if Jesus Christ has actually conquered the grave"? What makes *you* fearful?

4. Are you more likely to be "too heavenly minded to do earthly good" or the other way around—"too earthly minded to do heavenly good"?

5. Which of your neighbors do you have the hardest time loving? Why might your neighbors sometimes have a hard time loving you?

6. How concerned are you by polarization and fragmentation in American society? Do you see the same problem in the church? What is causing it? Take some time to lament any polarization you see in or around your own life.

7. At the end of the chapter Chris says he's "sure you're wishing I'd said more about some particular way that we twenty-first-century Christians are failing to love God and our neighbors as we ought." Ask each person in your group to either reiterate something that resonated with them in this chapter or suggest a different way that we are failing to love God and our neighbors.

Chapter 2: Hoping for Better Times
PRAY passages: Psalm 22:1-5, 27-31; 1 Peter 1:3-9

1. Pray the prayer Jesus taught his disciples in Matthew 6:9-13, often called the Lord's Prayer or the Our Father. As you pray, "Your kingdom come. Your will be done," envision it as a prayer God can and will answer today, rather than one God will answer only on the day of Christ's return. How does praying in this way change both the prayer and your outlook?

2. How does your faith in God lead you to lean toward hope for a better future for the church and the world?

3. Michelle Clifton-Soderstrom writes, "The heavenly kingdom . . . is the blueprint from which we build." What are some key characteristics of God's heavenly kingdom you would like to see serve as a blueprint for our priorities and efforts as Christians in today's world?

4. Mark shares the story of his Armenian grandmother, who fled genocide, as an example of someone from whom he learned about the power of hope. What are some stories from your family, church, or community that help you understand what it means to live as a person of hope?

5. Living in a broken world, how can hope help us to notice the good? How does it encourage us to more boldly participate in God's loving activity in the world?

6. If you agree that a better future for us and our world is "one in which God's people are becoming more Christ-like," how can you more intentionally pursue this goal? Who can you look to for support in this pursuit? Name some names and next steps.

7. Mark writes, "Choosing to trust God is a recurrent necessity for us, as it was for Abraham and Sarah and everyone who has walked by faith since." Amid your life's challenges and choices, what are some specific ways God is leading you to walk by faith?

Chapter 3: A More Extensive Listening to the Word of God
PRAY passage: Psalm 1

1. The paper "Biblical Authority and Christian Freedom" states, "To read [the Bible] properly . . . is to find it an altar where one meets the living God and receives personally the reality of redemption." Have you ever felt like you met the living God while reading the Bible? Is this kind of encounter with God something you pray would happen as you read the Bible?

2. In what ways do you currently present yourself "to the Scriptures' powerful influence"? Where or to whom can you look for ideas and encouragement to do so more fully?

3. In what ways do you think reading and studying the Bible with others is important, even transformative? Is this something you do? If not, how might it be beneficial to do so?

4. What are some key theological, biblical, and social issues on which Christians are divided? Which are essential to salvation? Which are important yet not essential to salvation? And which do you think are a matter of personal preference or perspective?

5. What is an example of a time you listened carefully and respectfully to someone whose experience or perspective was different from yours? When have you prayed and studied the Bible with people who held different views? How could you go about doing this?

6. Which, if any, elements of the PRAY (Pray, Repent, Ask, Yes) acronym are already a part of how you approach the Bible? Which ones would you like to incorporate more?

7. In what ways are you like the younger brother in Jesus' parable in Luke 15:11-32, who wandered away and squandered the opportunities and resources given him? How are you like the older brother, striving and committed yet tempted to be critical and judgmental of yourself and others?

8. As our heavenly Father looks at you right now, what is the expression on his face? Can you imagine his arms wide open, inviting you to let him love you? In what direction is God inviting you to walk with him?

Chapter 4: The Common Priesthood for the Common Good
PRAY passages: James 1:19-27; Hebrews 10:19-25

1. Have you heard the church described as a common priesthood (or priesthood of all believers)? Do you think of yourself as a priest? What would change if you did think in those terms?

2. Does "common priesthood" as Spener meant it describe your congregation? If not, where does the ideal get lost? What would it take to recover this priesthood in your faith community, and what benefits would that bring?

3. Are you comfortable with the language of personal and social holiness? Why or why not?

4. What do you think of Dale Brown's notion of "Christ the Servant of culture"? Would following that model change how you think about politics? Work and career? Family?

5. Pietists often use the language of seeking "God's glory and neighbors' good." Do you think Carl Lundquist is right that "social action" flows out of "personal devotion to Christ"? How do you see those two goals related to each other? Can one distract from the other?

6. "Compassion and justice," Chris argues, "are causes and effects of each other in the kingdom of God." Can you think of examples of this relationship (or of Brown's observation that those who serve compassionately are moved to combat injustice)?

Chapter 5: Christianity as Life

PRAY passages: Colossians 3:1-17; John 3:1-21

1. According to the Pietists, a living Christian faith is one in which the head, heart, and hands are all fully engaged. Is there one of the three you tend to lean toward more heavily? Is there one you could engage more fully?

2. What devotional practices have you found helpful for your inward journey? In what ways would you like to further develop your devotional life?

3. How does looking to Jesus shape the way you look at others, especially those you find most difficult to like, love, and relate to? How does praying for others help change the way you see them?

4. Do you meet with others to encourage one another in your inward and outward journey? If you do, how can you better encourage one another in both journeys? If you don't, whom could you partner with?

5. Mark suggests that many of us too often allow ourselves to be stirred up to "fear, emotional reactivity, and hate" rather than to "love and good deeds," as Hebrews 10:24 exhorts us. What stirs you up in a negative direction? How can you better encourage yourself and others in a more positive, God-trusting, God-honoring direction?

6. How does following Jesus' path of love "entail more vulnerability, not less"? What are ways Jesus' example and teaching challenge you to risk going beyond what is comfortable to love God and neighbor?

7. Mark writes that "expressing our love for Jesus by turning our attention toward our neighbors is imperative." What do the stories about Jesus and told by Jesus tell us about where we should focus our loving attention? Who are the neighbors God is calling you to love? What would loving them entail?

Chapter 6: The Irenic Spirit
PRAY passages: John 17; Philippians 2:1-11

1. At a formative stage in his life, Chris experienced several examples of Christian disunity. Have you been part of a church split? What caused it? In hindsight, do you think it was unavoidable or necessary?

2. Chris wonders whether "common experience and common activity are healthier bases for unity than common belief." Do you agree? What would a unity centered on experience or activity look like?

3. Chris quotes the Evangelical Covenant statement that mission consists, at least in part, of "the befriending of others . . . in the name of the One who first befriended us." Do you think about mission in terms of "befriending"? How would this view change how you and your community approach mission, or how you think about the importance of Christian unity?

4. Have you experienced something like the *synaspismos* Andy Crouch describes in your congregation? If this kind of unity were the "complicated *eikon*" that your church and other nearby churches showed to the world, how would things be different?

5. As you think about your own church or denomination, do you see a meaningful distinction between unity and uniformity? In practice, how might your faith community strive for both diversity and unity?

6. What's an example of an issue where you feel that it's appropriate for a Christian to say, "Here I stand; I can do no other"? On what issues do you think Christians *can* do other—or at least patiently continue to engage in conversation with a fellow believer who holds a different viewpoint?

7. Close by asking and praying over some of the questions that conclude the chapter. Is your church forming people for Christian unity?

Chapter 7: Whole-Person, Whole-Life Formation
PRAY passages: Romans 12:1-2; Philippians 1:9-11

1. Get started by reflecting on your experience of Christian formation, in and out of the church. If you're in a small group, let everyone share some stories.

2. What would it mean to live a life centered on Jesus Christ? Would you answer this question differently if you emphasized Jesus more than Christ or vice versa?

3. In their book on higher education, Chris and his colleagues celebrated virtues such as love, hope, humility, hospitality, and open-mindedness as the markers of transformation. Have you grown in these virtues? If so, what led to this growth? What are some other markers of Christian formation?

4. Do you learn more by individual study or in community with other people? If it's some of each, how do they relate to each other?

5. How does your church approach Christian formation? Is there continuity in goals and emphases, or does Christian formation look very different at each stage of life?

6. Do you think Chris is right that there are aspects of formational ministries that, while necessary and important, can distract from a centering focus on Jesus? If so, what are some examples, and what could be done about them?

7. Chris primarily discusses colleges and seminaries and then children, youth, and family ministry in this chapter. How might you apply the same principles to adult ministries or to parenting?

Chapter 8: Proclaiming the Good News

PRAY passages: Acts 10:34-43; Romans 10:1-17

1. Mark says a critical factor in proclaiming the gospel is that "we must be experiencing it ourselves as good news if we hope to share it as such." What are ways you have experienced God's love in your life?

2. Mark writes that it is crucial for pastors to bring an "expectant faith" to their preaching, sermon preparation, devotional times, and all that they do. How does such an expectant faith make a difference, for pastors or for anyone else?

3. What makes for a good sermon, from your point of view? How about a good listener to a sermon? In what ways can or do you invite sermons to "penetrate to the heart" and make a difference in how you live?

4. When have you experienced listening as a more meaningful act of love than speaking, whether you've been on the giving or receiving end of the action? In what situations might loving through listening be something you need to practice more?

5. Whom could you try to love better by choosing to listen more without being anxious or judgmental, or trying to fix anything?

6. Is sharing your faith with others something you'd like to do? What is it about sharing your faith that is difficult for you? What about your relationship with God is such a gift to you that you would love to see others experience that gift too?

7. Who in your circle of relationships is God nudging you to pray would awaken to God's love? What are some ways you could be a part of the answer to that prayer?

Notes

Introduction: "Come Back to Jesus"

3 *scholars even suggest connections*: For example, Valerie C. Cooper, "Equality in an Age of Inequality: Pietism in Nineteenth-Century African American Thought," *The Covenant Quarterly*, August–November 2012, 21-34; Roger E. Olson, "Pietism and Pentecostalism: Spiritual Cousins or Competitors?," *Pneuma* 34 (2012): 319-44.

the main form of Protestantism: Roger E. Olson, *The Story of Christian Theology: Twenty Centuries of Tradition and Reform* (Downers Grove, IL: InterVarsity Press, 1999), 491.

had almost vanished in America: "Pietism," *Wikipedia*, https://en.wikipedia .org/wiki/Pietism, accessed April 4, 2017.

4 *describes Pietism as "leavening"*: Steven M. Nolt, "Critical Reflections," in *Becoming Grace: Seventy-Five Years on the Landscape of Christian Higher Education in America*, ed. Jared S. Burkholder and M. M. Norris (Winona Lake, IN: BMH Books, 2015), 213.

transcends denominations and even traditions: Roger E. Olson and Christian T. Collins Winn, *Reclaiming Pietism: Retrieving an Evangelical Tradition* (Grand Rapids: Eerdmans, 2015), 9, 71.

superficial Christianity whether it be found: Virgil A. Olson, "The Baptist General Conference and Its Pietistic Heritage," *Bethel Seminary Quarterly* 4 (May 1956): 65.

5 *its current president rarely misses a chance*: For example, Gary Walter, "Who We Are at Our Best," *The Covenant Companion*, March 2010, 5.

6 *was a rekindling of the love affair*: Alec Ryrie, *Protestants: The Faith That Made the Modern World* (New York: Viking, 2017), 167.

8 *O it is a living, busy, active, mighty thing*: Martin Luther, "Preface to the Epistle of St. Paul to the Romans" (1523), in *Luther's Works*, vol. 35, ed. E. Theodore Bachmann (Philadelphia: Muhlenberg Press, 1960), 370.

9   *not inherited or assumed*: Christopher Gehrz, "Does Pietism Provide a 'Usable Past' for Christian Colleges and Universities?," in *The Pietist Vision of Christian Higher Education: Forming Whole and Holy Persons*, ed. Christopher Gehrz (Downers Grove, IL: IVP Academic, 2015), 20.

     hold together proclamation and compassion: Evangelical Covenant Church, *Covenant Affirmations*, rev. ed. (Chicago: Covenant Publications, 2005), 11, 13.

10   *With sincere devotion*: Philip Jacob Spener, *Pia Desideria* (1675), trans. and ed. Theodore G. Tappert (Philadelphia: Fortress, 1964), 38.

11   *Pietist not just in content but tone*: Gehrz, "Does Pietism Provide a 'Usable Past,'" 30-31.

     Pietists have been sharing personal testimonies: Johanna Eleonora Petersen, *The Life of Lady Johanna Eleonora Petersen, Written by Herself: Pietism and Women's Autobiography in Seventeenth-Century Germany*, ed. and trans. Barbara Becker-Cantarino (Chicago: University of Chicago Press, 2005).

1 What's Wrong?

15   *Hopeful as he was*: Philip Jacob Spener, *Pia Desideria* (1675), ed. and trans. Theodore G. Tappert (Philadelphia: Fortress, 1964), 39.

     "corrupt conditions" that Spener decried: Ibid., 40, 43.

16   *the complaints of godly people*: Ibid., 73.

17   *Just as the seed strewn*: August Hermann Francke, "The Doctrine of Our Lord Jesus Christ Concerning Rebirth" (1697), quoted in Gary R. Sattler, *God's Glory, Neighbor's Good: A Brief Introduction to the Life and Writings of August Hermann Francke* (Chicago: Covenant Press, 1982), 141-42.

     Chastise yourself first: August Hermann Francke, "Scriptural Rules of Life" (1695), in Sattler, *God's Glory, Neighbor's Good*, 204.

18   *authentic sabbath keeping*: Lauren F. Winner, *Mudhouse Sabbath: An Invitation to a Life of Spiritual Discipline* (Brewster, MA: Paraclete, 2003), 11-13.

     advice from an eighteenth-century Pietist: John Frederick Stark, *Daily Hand-Book for Days of Rejoicing and of Sorrow* (1728; trans. and repr., Philadelphia: Kohler, 1879), 10, 28.

19   *functional atheism*: Parker J. Palmer, *Let Your Life Speak: Listening for the Voice of Vocation* (San Francisco: Jossey-Bass, 2000), 88.

     sabbath commemorates: Winner, *Mudhouse Sabbath*, 12.

     which issues were "very important": Pew Research Center, "Evangelicals Rally to Trump, Religious 'Nones' Back Clinton," July 13, 2016, www.pewforum

.org/2016/07/13/religion-and-the-2016-campaign/#religious-groups-agree
-economy-terrorism-are-key-election-concerns.

19   *chances of an American being killed*: Alex Nowratseh, "Americans' Fear of
Foreign Terrorists Is Overinflated," *Time*, September 13, 2016, http://time
.com/4489405/americans-fear-of-foreign-terrorists.

21   *awaken a fervent love*: Spener, *Pia Desideria*, 96.

Faith brings you to Christ: Martin Luther, sermon on Matthew 21:1-9 (1522),
quoted in Michelle A. Clifton-Soderstrom, *Angels, Worms, and Bogeys: The
Christian Ethic of Pietism* (Eugene, OR: Cascade, 2010), 68.

some Lutherans let their aversion: August Hermann Francke, "Duty to the
Poor" (1697), in Sattler, *God's Glory, Neighbor's Good*, 158.

the echo of a voice: N. T. Wright, *Simply Christian: Why Christianity Makes
Sense* (New York: HarperOne, 2006), 3.

American Values Survey: Betsy Cooper, Daniel Cox, Rachel Lienesch, and
Robert P. Jones, "Anxiety, Nostalgia, and Mistrust: Findings from the 2015
American Values Survey," Public Religion Research Institute, November 17,
2015, www.prri.org/research/survey-anxiety-nostalgia-and-mistrust-findings
-from-the-2015-american-values-survey.

22   *blinding themselves to the injustices faced*: Russell Moore, "A White Church
No More," *New York Times*, May 6, 2016, www.nytimes.com/2016/05/06/
opinion/a-white-church-no-more.html?_r=0.

Many white evangelicals: Russell Moore, "What Shootings and Racial Justice
Mean for the Body of Christ," personal website, July 7, 2016, www.russelmoore
.com/2016/07/07/shootings-justice-body-of-christ.

Christianity's best gift to the world: Philip Yancey, *What's So Amazing About
Grace?* (Grand Rapids: Zondervan, 1997), 30, 84.

23   *interprets the Isak Dinesen story "Babette's Feast"*: Ibid., 26.

the remarkable Johanna Eleonora Petersen: Clifton-Soderstrom, *Angels,
Worms, and Bogeys*, 63.

Fear, for [Pietists], was never about: interview with C. John Weborg in ibid., 105.

One of Jesus' clearest teachings: Ibid., 50-51.

24   *this dismal summary*: Paul Taylor, "The Demographic Trends Shaping
American Politics in 2016 and Beyond," Pew Research Center, January 27,
2016, www.pewresearch.org/fact-tank/2016/01/27/the-demographic-trends
-shaping-american-politics-in-2016-and-beyond.

24   *over 60 percent of voters lived*: David Wasserman, "Purple America Has All But Disappeared," *FiveThirtyEight*, March 8, 2017, http://fivethirtyeight.com/features/purple-america-has-all-but-disappeared.

25   *Evangelical leaders including*: "Letter to President Trump on Executive Order on Refugees," World Vision, January 2017, www.worldvision.org/about-us/media-center/letter-president-trump-executive-order-refugees.

     76 percent of white evangelicals: Pew Research Center, "Views of Trump's Executive Order on Travel Restrictions," February 16, 2017, www.people-press.org/2017/02/16/2-views-of-trumps-executive-order-on-travel-restrictions.

     "My love," understood Johanna Petersen: Quoted in Clifton-Soderstrom, *Angels, Worms, and Bogeys*, 58.

2 Hoping for Better Times

27   *In the resurrection of Jesus*: Kyle A. Roberts, "Eschatology and Hope," in *Dictionary of Christian Spirituality*, ed. Glen G. Scorgie et al. (Grand Rapids: Zondervan, 2011), 89.

28   *in a time of extreme challenges*: See, for example, Geoffrey Parker and Lesley M. Smith, eds., *The General Crisis of the Seventeenth Century*, 2nd ed. (London: Routledge, 1997).

     Above all, [Spener] hoped: Dale W. Brown, *Understanding Pietism*, rev. ed. (Nappanee, IN: Evangel, 1996), 85-86.

29   *We are not living in a Platonic state*: Philip Jacob Spener, *Pia Desideria* (1675), ed. and trans. Theodore G. Tappert (Philadelphia: Fortress, 1964), 80.

30   *active expectation*: See Christoph Blumhardt, *Action in Waiting* (Walden, NY: Plough, 1998).

     the Pietists' hope was both: Michelle A. Clifton-Soderstrom, *Angels, Worms, and Bogeys: The Christian Ethic of Pietism* (Eugene, OR: Cascade, 2010), 88.

31   *Those who hope build*: Ibid., 87-89.

     In the power of the resurrection: Roberts, "Eschatology and Hope," 93-94.

32   *to God's glory and neighbor's good*: Francke used this phrase multiple times throughout his writings and sermons; he borrowed it from the Heidelberg Catechism (1563), Q&A 101.

35   *including the Great Awakenings*: On the influence of Pietism on the awakenings of the eighteenth century, see W. R. Ward, *The Protestant Evangelical Awakening* (Cambridge: Cambridge University Press, 1992).

3 A More Extensive Listening to the Word of God

41 *the powerful means*: Philip Jacob Spener, *Pia Desideria* (1675), ed. and trans. Theodore G. Tappert (Philadelphia: Fortress, 1964), 87; emphasis added.

42 *The more at home the Word of God*: Ibid.

    This much is certain: Ibid., 91.

43 *an altar where one meets the living God*: Covenant Committee on Freedom and Theology, "Biblical Authority and Christian Freedom," Evangelical Covenant Church, June 18, 1963, 5; available from the Frisk Collection of Covenant Literature (North Park University), http://collections.carli .illinois.edu/cdm/ref/collection/npu_swecc/id/36987.

44 *we still love [the Bible]*: Kenneth A. Briggs, interview by Emily McFarlan Miller, "Veteran Religion Reporter Looks for the Bible in Public Life," Religion News Service, September 7, 2016, http://religionnews.com/2016/09/07 /veteran-religion-reporter-looks-for-the-bible-in-public-life-in-new-book.

    altogether different people: Spener, *Pia Desideria*, 91.

    Our modern interest in understanding the context: On Pietist contributions to biblical scholarship, see Douglas A. Shantz, *An Introduction to German Pietism: Protestant Renewal at the Dawn of Modern Europe* (Baltimore: Johns Hopkins University Press, 2013), chap. 8.

45 *Do not seek to measure*: A. H. Francke, "Scriptural Rules of Life" (1695), in Gary R. Sattler, *God's Glory, Neighbor's Good: A Brief Introduction to the Life and Writings of August Hermann Francke* (Chicago: Covenant Press, 1982), 223.

    Most of our history has been: Briggs, in "Veteran Religion Reporter Looks for the Bible."

46 *The spiritual power of the pietist movement*: "Biblical Authority and Christian Freedom," 5.

    Christian vitality has not always been: Ibid., 13.

50 *One thing we miss*: Briggs, in "Veteran Religion Reporter Looks for the Bible."

    Exegetically, Spener and Francke differed: Dale W. Brown, *Understanding Pietism*, rev. ed. (Nappanee, IN: Evangel, 1996), 48.

    In a guide for reading the Scriptures: Philipp Jakob Spener, "The Necessary and Useful Reading of the Holy Scriptures" (1694), in *The Pietists: Selected Writings*, ed. Peter C. Erb (New York: Paulist Press, 1983), 71-72.

51 *As Luther wrote*: Quoted in Erb, *Pietists*, 72.

52 *Now before you, Lord*: Lina Sandell, "Now Before You, Lord, We Gather," trans. A. L. Skoog, in *The Covenant Hymnal: A Worshipbook* (Chicago: Covenant Publications, 1996), #500.

54 *Accordingly all Scripture*: Spener, *Pia Desideria*, 88.

   Belief in the Bible's power: Evangelical Covenant Church, "The Evangelical Covenant Church and the Bible," Covenant Resource Paper, 2008, www .covchurch.org/wp-content/uploads/sites/2/2010/05/Covenant-Resource -Paper.pdf.

56 *If as individual Christians*: "Biblical Authority and Christian Freedom," 7.

4 The Common Priesthood for the Common Good

The first two paragraphs of this chapter are adapted from one of Chris's contributions to "Covenanters Reading Scripture Through History," Evangelical Covenant Church (2016), http://cbe.covchurch.org/wp-content/uploads/2016/08/Covenant -History-and-Heritage-CBE.pdf. Used by permission of the ECC.

57 *these Pietists "gathered"*: Glen Wiberg, *This Side of the River: A Centennial Story, Salem Covenant Church, 1888–1988* (New Brighton, MN: Salem Covenant Church, 1995), 75.

58 *There is probably nothing in which historians*: Dale W. Brown, *Understanding Pietism*, rev. ed. (Nappanee, IN: Evangel, 1996), 86-87.

   a quiet conventicle-Christianity: Robert Friedmann, *Mennonite Piety Through the Centuries: Its Genius and Its Literature* (Goshen, IN: Mennonite Historical Society, 1949), 11.

   the establishment and diligent exercise: Philip Jacob Spener, *Pia Desideria* (1675), ed. and trans. Theodore G. Tappert (Philadelphia: Fortress, 1964), 92-93.

   the common priesthood seeking the common good: I'm borrowing this phrase from my former Bethel colleague and now Covenant church planter Dale Durie, who made it the title of his chapter in *The Pietist Vision of Christian Higher Education: Forming Whole and Holy Persons*, ed. Christopher Gehrz (Downers Grove, IL: IVP Academic, 2015), 109-22.

   Let everyone, therefore: Martin Luther, *On the Babylonian Captivity of the Church* (1520), quoted in Jonathan Strom, "The Common Priesthood and the Pietist Challenge for Ministry and Laity," in *The Pietist Impulse in Christianity*, ed. Christian T. Collins Winn et al. (Eugene, OR: Pickwick, 2011), 43.

58-59   *all Christians without distinction*: Phillip Jakob Spener, "The Spiritual Priesthood" (1677), in *The Pietists: Selected Writings*, ed. Emilie Griffin and Peter C. Erb (New York: HarperSanFrancisco, 2006), 3, 17.

59   *prefers common priesthood*: See Strom, "Common Priesthood and the Pietist Challenge," 42-62.

    Increasingly dissatisfied with the hierarchical church: Hank Voss, *The Priesthood of All Believers and the* Missio Dei: *A Canonical, Catholic, and Contextual Approach* (Eugene, OR: Pickwick, 2016), 132-33.

    priesthood entailed three specific duties: Spener, "Spiritual Priesthood," 4-13.

60   *the practice of faith was so limited*: Michelle A. Clifton-Soderstrom, *Angels, Worms, and Bogeys: The Christian Ethic of Pietism* (Eugene, OR: Cascade, 2010), 66.

    Francke was even more pointed: A. H. Francke, quoted in Brown, *Understanding Pietism*, 42.

61   *sets leaders and followers up for failure*: Jen Hatmaker, "How a Consumer Culture Threatens to Destroy Pastors," Acts of Faith, *The Washington Post*, September 8, 2015, www.washingtonpost.com/news/acts-of-faith/wp/2015 /09/08/how-a-consumer-culture-threatens-to-destroy-pastors.

    the ministry cannot accomplish: Spener, *Pia Desideria*, 94.

    everyone must preach with their lives: C. O. Rosenius, "Spiritual Priesthood" (1843), in *The Swedish Pietists: Excerpts from the Writings of Carl Olof Rosenius and Paul Peter Waldenström*, ed. and trans. Mark Safstrom (Eugene, OR: Pickwick, 2015), 110.

62   *When we come before God*: Mark Pattie, "Send Me!," sermon preached at Salem Covenant Church, New Brighton, MN, May 31, 2015.

    Solitary Religion is not to be found: John and Charles Wesley, *Hymns and Sacred Poems* (London: William Strahan, 1739), viii.

63   *greatest joy to be occupied*: Spener, "Spiritual Priesthood," 13.

    transformers of culture: H. Richard Niebuhr, *Christ and Culture* (New York: Harper & Row, 1951), 191.

64   *the pietistic Christianity he had known*: Dale Brown, "Anabaptism and Pietism" (talk at Elizabethtown College, 1990), quoted in Christopher Gehrz, "Missional Pietists: Lessons from Dale W. Brown and Carl H. Lundquist," *Covenant Quarterly*, August–November 2012, 37-41.

    I like to think that these bold and serious-minded: Perry Engle, "Bold, Sweetened, with a Little Bit of Room," *In Part*, December 17, 2012, http:// inpart.org/dept/parting-words/bold-sweetened-little-bit-room.

65 *Lundquist once preached*: Carl H. Lundquist, 1969 and 1970 annual reports to the Baptist General Conference, quoted in Gehrz, "Missional Pietists," 42-45. Lundquist is quoting Donald G. Bloesch, *The Crisis of Piety: Essays Towards a Theology of the Christian Life* (Grand Rapids: Eerdmans, 1968), 48.

As a result of the emphasis on the love: Brown, *Understanding Pietism*, 97.

carries out his professional calling joyfully: A. H. Francke, "Scriptural and Basic Introduction to True Christianity" (date uncertain), in Gary R. Sattler, *God's Glory, Neighbor's Good: A Brief Introduction to the Life and Writings of August Hermann Francke* (Chicago: Covenant Press, 1982), 253.

if you cannot turn your profession: A. H. Francke, "Scriptural Rules of Life" (1699), in Sattler, *God's Glory, Neighbor's Good*, 230.

a Band-Aid approach: Brown, *Understanding Pietism*, 97.

66 *We also confess that*: Covenant Resource Paper, "The Evangelical Covenant Church and the Ministry of Compassion, Mercy, and Justice," adopted 2011, www.covchurch.org/wp-content/uploads/sites/2/2011/01/35.-Covenant -Resource-Paper-CMJ-5.17.pdf.

Some churches preach truth: Efrem Smith, "Truth, Justice, and Righteousness," Missio Alliance, August 9, 2009, www.missioalliance.org/truth -justice-and-righteousness.

Those who put on Band-Aids: Brown, *Understanding Pietism*, 97.

67 *Pietist impulse to extend the care*: Christian T. Collins Winn, "Groaning for the Kingdom of God: Spirituality, Social Justice, and the Witness of the Blumhardts," *Journal of Spiritual Formation & Soul Care* 6 (Spring 2013): 58.

Carl Lundquist encouraged: Carl H. Lundquist, "Enduring Values of the Renewal Movement" (unpublished report, 1976), quoted in Gehrz, "Missional Pietists," 43-45.

5 Christianity as Life

68 *Christianity is essentially a personal relationship*: Donald C. Frisk, *The New Life in Christ* (Chicago: Covenant Press, 1969), xi-xii.

69 *It is by no means enough*: Philip Jacob Spener, *Pia Desideria* (1675), ed. and trans. Theodore G. Tappert (Philadelphia: Fortress, 1964), 95.

70 *"religious experience" simply for*: Frisk, *New Life in Christ*, xii.

Lutheran orthodoxy treated faith: Gary R. Sattler, *God's Glory, Neighbor's Good: A Brief Introduction to the Life and Writings of August Hermann Francke* (Chicago: Covenant Press, 1982), 105.

71 *When they hear the gospel*: Martin Luther, preface to *Commentary on Romans*, quoted in Spener, *Pia Desideria*, 64-65.

   heart ready to do the divine will: C. John Weborg, "Scripture Demands More," *Covenant Companion*, September 5, 2016, http://covenantcompanion .com/2016/09/05/scripture-demands-more.

72 *Faith, however, is a divine work*: Luther, preface to *Romans*, quoted in Spener, *Pia Desideria*, 64-65.

   Our dear Savior repeatedly: Spener, *Pia Desideria*, 95.

73 *awaken a fervent love among*: Ibid., 96.

   Teach me, where'er Thy steps I see: Nicholas von Zinzendorf, "O Thou, to Whose All-Searching Sight," trans. John Wesley, *Hymnal and Liturgies of the Moravian Church* (Chicago: Moravian Church in America, 1969), #481.

   were concerned first and foremost in cultivating: Mark Safstrom, ed. and trans., *The Swedish Pietists: Excerpts from the Writings of Carl Olof Rosenius and Paul Peter Waldenström* (Eugene, OR: Pickwick, 2015), 7.

74 *Prayer is to look to*: Letter from Gerhard Tersteegen, December 4, 1731, in *The Pietists: Selected Writings*, ed. Emilie Griffin and Peter C. Erb (New York: HarperSanFrancisco, 2006), 122.

75 *accustom the people first to work on*: Spener, *Pia Desideria*, 116-17.

76 *Over the years I met*: Richard Rohr, "The Activist's Guide to Contemplation," *Sojourners*, May 23, 2016, https://sojo.net/articles/activists-guide -contemplation.

77 *Whatever form conversion takes*: Frisk, *New Life in Christ*, 18. Emphasis original.

   All the commandments are summed up: Spener, *Pia Desideria*, 96.

79 *Neighbors who had known each other*: Susan Pattie, "When Neighbors Become Enemies: Armenian Identities Constructed, Deconstructed, Reconstructed," talk given at the University of Michigan, October 2016.

   If there appears to be doubt: Spener, *Pia Desideria*, 97.

6 The Irenic Spirit

83 *With a modesty born of confidence*: Evangelical Covenant Church, *Covenant Affirmations*, rev. ed. (Chicago: Covenant Publications, 2005), 19.

84 *even if arguing about doctrine*: Philip Jacob Spener, *Pia Desideria* (1675), ed. and trans. Theodore G. Tappert (Philadelphia: Fortress, 1964), 101-2.

   If there is any prospect: Ibid., 99.

84 *the duty and wisdom of every Christian*: C. O. Rosenius, "The Diversity of God's Children" (1859), in *The Swedish Pietists: Excerpts from the Writings of Carl Olof Rosenius and Paul Peter Waldenström*, ed. and trans. Mark Safstrom (Eugene, OR: Pickwick, 2015), 116.

We love to understand pietism: George Scott and C. O. Rosenius, "Pietism" (1842), in Safstrom, *Swedish Pietists*, 34.

85 *Unity as Mission*: This section is adapted from Chris Gehrz, "Invitation to a Stranger," *Pietisten* 31 (Fall/Winter 2016), http://pietisten.org/xxxi/2 /invitation.html. Used by permission of the publisher.

At the end of his life, Jesus: Evangelical Covenant Church, *Covenant Affirmations*, 12.

86 *Unity as Witness*: This section is adapted from Chris Gehrz, "What We Mean When We Say We Want Christian Unity," *Mennonite World Review*, August 28, 2015, http://mennoworld.org/2015/08/28/the-world-together/what -we-mean-when-we-say-we-want-christian-unity. Used by permission of the publisher.

87 *tells of visiting an Eastern Orthodox monastery*: Andy Crouch, *Playing God: Redeeming the Gift of Power* (Downers Grove, IL: InterVarsity Press, 2013), 94-97.

88 *In the Christian congregation*: Paul Peter Waldenström, "The People of God Is One Body" (1904), in Safstrom, *Swedish Pietists*, 108.

for the sake of maintaining unity: David Gushee, "The Great Evangelical Divorce: Continuing the Conversation," Religion News Service, February 15, 2016, http://religionnews.com/2016/02/15/conservative-progressive-evangelical -divorce-qa.

89 *at great risk of engaging in groupthink*: Christena Cleveland, *Disunity in Christ: Uncovering the Hidden Forces That Keep Us Apart* (Downers Grove, IL: InterVarsity Press, 2013), 42.

Since we have a tendency: Rosenius, "Diversity of God's Children," 116.

Peace within the group does not mean: C. J. Nyvall, *Travel Memories from America* (1876), trans. E. Gustav Johnson (Chicago: Covenant Press, 1959), 20.

brings forth a rich variety of gifts: Pope Francis, *Evangelii Gaudium*, Vatican Press, November 2013, http://w2.vatican.va/content/francesco/en /apost_exhortations/documents/papa-francesco_esortazione-ap_20131124 _evangelii-gaudium.html.

there is space to delight in the variety: Kathy Khang, "Rice Pudding and Other Cross-Cultural Adventures as an Outsider," KathyKhang.com,

October 24, 2012, www.kathykhang.com/2012/10/24/rice-pudding-and -other-cross-cultural-adventures-as-an-outsider.

91 *Everyone receives spiritual formation*: Dallas Willard, *The Great Omission: Reclaiming Jesus's Essential Teachings on Discipleship* (New York: HarperSan-Francisco, 2006), 69.

7 Whole-Person, Whole-Life Formation

95 *center from which radiates*: David Nyvall, "The Poetry of Missions" (1901), quoted in Scott E. Erickson, "David Nyvall and the Shape of an Immigrant Church: Ethnic, Denominational, and Educational Priorities Among Swedes in America" (doctoral dissertation, University of Uppsala, 1996), 267.

nurseries of the church: Philip Jacob Spener, *Pia Desideria* (1675), ed. and trans. Theodore G. Tappert (Philadelphia: Fortress, 1964), 103, 104.

96 *its great comfort with "Jesus" talk*: Phyllis Tickle, foreword to *The Pietists: Selected Writings*, ed. Emilie Griffin and Peter C. Erb (New York: Harper-SanFrancisco, 2006), viii-ix.

the unifying center: Carl H. Lundquist, 1959 annual report to the Baptist General Conference, quoted in Christopher Gehrz, "Recovering a Pietist Understanding of Christian Higher Education: Carl H. Lundquist and Karl A. Olsson," *Christian Scholar's Review* 40 (Winter 2011): 146.

He has become the supreme affection: Carl H. Lundquist, "Bethel as Community," *(Baptist General Conference) Standard*, October 5, 1970, 16.

97 *the faith which underlies*: Karl A. Olsson, "The Idea of a Christian School" (1959) and "The Meaning of Comprehensive Education" (1961), quoted in Gehrz, "Recovering a Pietist Understanding," 145-46. For more on Olsson at North Park, see Kurt W. Peterson and R. J. Snell, "'Faith Forms the Intellectual Task': The Pietist Option in Christian Higher Education," in *The Pietist Impulse in Christianity*, ed. Christian T. Collins Winn et al. (Eugene, OR: Pickwick, 2011), 215-30.

The modern scientist of pietistic background: Richard W. Peterson, "Pietist Values in Science and Science Education," in *The Pietist Vision of Christian Higher Education: Forming Whole and Holy Persons*, ed. Christopher Gehrz (Downers Grove, IL: IVP Academic, 2015), 152-53.

In the uncertain and perhaps bizarre: Karl A. Olsson, "Charge to the Graduates," June 13, 1965, Olsson Presidential Papers, Box 15, Covenant Archives, Chicago.

begins with the experience of knowing: Roger E. Olson, "Reconceiving the Christ-Centered College: Convertive Piety and Life Together," in Gehrz, *Pietist Vision*, 100.

98   *endows his existence*: Olsson, "Idea of a Christian School," quoted in Gehrz, "Recovering a Pietist Understanding," 146.

will leave one altered: David Williams, "Pietism and Faith-Learning Integration in the Evangelical University," in Gehrz, *Pietist Vision*, 45.

education is linked not only: Olsson, "Meaning of Comprehensive Education," quoted in Gehrz, "Recovering a Pietist Understanding," 145; emphasis added.

when one's whole person is involved: Williams, "Pietism and Faith-Learning Integration," 45; emphasis added.

to glorify God and form persons: Olson, "Reconceiving the Christ-Centered College," 101; emphasis added.

99   *What Pietists advocated*: Katherine J. Nevins, "Calling for Pietistic Community: *Pia Desideria* in the Classroom," in Gehrz, *Pietist Vision*, 53, 63.

form "men and women for others:" This phrase from Pedro Arrupe is commonly used in Jesuit education; see "Education," Jesuits website, http://jesuits.org/whatwedo?PAGE=DTN-20130520123631.

a responsibility to extend learning: Marion H. Larson and Sara L. H. Shady, "Love My (Religious) Neighbor: A Pietist Approach to Christian Responsibility in a Pluralistic World," in Gehrz, *Pietist Vision*, 136-38. Larson and Shady have developed these ideas at greater length in *From Bubble to Bridge: Educating Christians for a Multifaith World* (Downers Grove, IL: IVP Academic, 2017).

100   *because such talk seems to come*: James K. A. Smith, *Desiring the Kingdom: Worship, Worldview, and Cultural Formation* (Grand Rapids: Baker Academic, 2009), 219n.

101   *In the end the impact of one life*: Lundquist, 1959 annual report, quoted in Gehrz, "Recovering a Pietist Understanding," 149.

Faith will be "stickier": See Kara E. Powell and Chap Clark, *Sticky Faith* (Grand Rapids: Zondervan, 2011).

102   *the letter of the heavenly Father*: Phillip Jakob Spener, "The Spiritual Priesthood" (1677), in Griffin and Erb, *The Pietists*, 7.

it is possible to believe the Bible: David Nyvall, quoted in Karl A. Olsson, *Into One Body . . . by the Cross*, vol. 1 (Chicago: Covenant Publications, 1985), 261.

Pietists loved the Bible: Roger E. Olson and Christian T. Collins Winn, *Reclaiming Pietism: Retrieving an Evangelical Tradition* (Grand Rapids: Eerdmans, 2015), 99.

103   *be conscious of a real conversion*: John Alexis Edgren, *Minnen från Havet, Kriget och Missionsfältet* (1878), quoted in Adolf Olson, *A Centenary History: As Related to the Baptist General Conference of America* (Chicago: Baptist Conference Press, 1952), 155.

At the center of everything: Olson, "Reconceiving the Christ-Centered College," 101.

the leadership of theologian John Weborg: In 1980 Weborg came to Bethel Seminary to give a talk that inspired many faculty to better incorporate spiritual formation into their work. Jeannette A. Bakke, "A Religion of the Heart and Bethel Seminary," *Baptist Pietist Clarion*, March 2012, 8.

104   *a servant of God's main purpose*: Olson and Collins Winn, *Reclaiming Pietism*, 183, 185.

It is imperative that faith: Donald Frisk, "Theological Perspectives for Christian Education" (1963), reprinted in *Pietisten* 28, no. 1 (Spring/Summer 2013), http://pietisten.org/xxviii/1/theological_perspective.html.

8 Proclaiming the Good News

105   *that sermons be so prepared*: Philip Jacob Spener, *Pia Desideria* (1675), ed. and trans. Theodore G. Tappert (Philadelphia: Fortress, 1964), 115.

106   *Certainly his lifestyle and actions*: Mark Galli, "Speak the Gospel," *Christianity Today*, May 21, 2009, www.christianitytoday.com/ct/2009/mayweb-only/120-42.0.html.

because the preacher has neglected: Gustaf F. Johnson, *Hearts Aflame* (1922), trans. Paul R. Johnson (Chicago: Covenant Publications, 1970), 8.

107   *it is not enough that we hear the Word*: Spener, *Pia Desideria*, 115-17.

109   *pleaded Caleb Kaltenbach*: Laurie Goodstein, "Evangelicals Open Door to Debate on Gay Rights," *New York Times*, June 8, 2015.

Another evangelical pastor told me: Personal communication; this story is used by permission.

There's absolutely ministry in it: Krista Tippett, interview with Katelyn Beaty, *Christianity Today*, July/August 2013, 36.

so often think they must always contribute: Dietrich Bonhoeffer, *Life Together* (New York: Harper & Row, 1954), 97-98.

110   *you have to make your vision apparent*: Flannery O'Connor, "The Fiction Writer and His Country," in *Mystery and Manners: Occasional Prose*, ed. Sally and Robert Fitzgerald (New York: Farrar, Straus & Giroux, 1969), 34.

111   *It is God's love for us*: Bonhoeffer, *Life Together*, 97.

112   *the first Protestant missionaries to India*: The mission to Tranquebar was just the beginning of Pietist missions in the eighteenth century. See Richard V. Pierard, "German Pietism as a Major Factor in the Beginnings of Modern Protestant Missions," in *The Pietist Impulse in Christianity*, ed. Christian T. Collins Winn et al. (Eugene, OR: Pickwick, 2011), 285-95.

113   *Growing up in church*: Glen V. Wiberg, *Housing the Sacred* (Chicago: Covenant Publications, 2009), 28.

      Evangelism is the spontaneous expression: Wesley W. Nelson, *Training for Evangelistic Visiting* (Chicago: Evangelical Covenant Church, 1978), 35.

Benediction: "Like a Tree Planted by Water"

117   *our late friend Glen Wiberg*: You can find Glen's 2015 memoir, *Born to Preach: To Intend Blessing*, at www.blurb.com/b/6673951-born-to-preach.

Name Index

Scripture Index